Keith Hill is a New Zealand writer whose work explores the intersection of spirituality, history, science, religion, mysticism and psychology. His books include *The God Revolution*, *Striving To Be Human*, and *Practical Spirituality*, each of which won the Ashton Wylie Award, New Zealand's premiere prize for spiritual writing.

Reviews of *The God Revolution*

"Hill's exposition is a fine example of scrupulously rigorous scholarship—it is remarkable how much ground is covered within his brief historical survey. ... An impressive and accessible introduction to a challenging philosophical topic. "—Kirkus Review

"Keith Hill is a writer in the vein of Karen Armstrong ... The prize that celebrates New Zealand's forward thinkers is thoroughly deserved."—Mike Alexander, Sunday Star Times

"A scholarly yet accessible book. ... Deserves to be read by all those who care about ideas, the trajectory of civilization and its future form." —Peter Dornauf, www.eyecontact.com

BOOKS BY KEITH HILL

NON-FICTION
The New Mysticism
The God Revolution
Experimental Spirituality
Practical Spirituality
Psychological Spirituality
What is Really Going On?
Where Do I Go When I Meditate?
How Did I End Up Here?

FICTION
The Ecstasy of Cabeza de Vaca
Puck of the Starways
Blue Kisses

CLASSICS OF WORLD MYSTICISM
The Bhagavad Gita: A New Poetic Version
I Cannot Live Without You:
Selected Poetry of Mirabai and Kabir
Psalms of Exile and Return
Interpretations of Desire:
Mystical Love Poems By Ibn 'Arabi

WITH PETER CALVERT
The Matapaua Conversations
The Kosmic Web

STRIVING TO BE HUMAN

How can we be moral in the modern world?

Keith Hill

attar‖books

First published by Attar Books 2011

Paperback ISBN 978-0-47319263-1
Ebook ISBN 978-0-9951059-5-9

Cover design by Abigail Kerr

Attar Books
www.attarbooks.com

CONTENTS

Introduction

This book examines the moral values we live by. In the past people tended to automatically adopt their forebears' moral values. In the majority of cultures those values were derived from religious beliefs, written up in sacred scriptures, and given authority by religious decree. Those same religiously derived moral values continue to remain fundamental in most nations today. However, in other ways outlooks have changed radically.

We no longer accept the views of our forebears as sacrosanct. Indeed, more often the opposite applies, and we view our ancestors' scientific, intellectual, technological, and cultural achievements and knowledge as inferior to our own. The majority of nations today are secular, not religious. In most science, technology, and economics have replaced religion as the social and intellectual drivers. And innumerable activities, such as splitting atoms, adding up balance sheets, and developing a new medicine, are not seen as having a religiously-derived moral dimension at all.

Nonetheless, most of us continue to consider that moral values have a role to play in our lives. Our moral sense leads us to ask questions such as whether that split atom will be used for war or peace, and whether either use is environmentally or socially acceptable. We debate whether the balance sheet created by the global economy is in social debit or credit, and what balance we should maintain between the health of the environment and the health of profits. Behind each of these questions is the larger consideration of what we should collectively value. Thus even in today's secular societies the question of moral values remains fundamental.

However, morality is also one area in our lives that we rarely examine closely. We tend to assume that the values we live by are right and true—and we're surprized to discover that others have very different values, yet think their values are equally right and true. Only occasionally do we reflect on how we came to live by the values we profess, and where they originated from.

In addition, the world has become a complex place. Globalization and information technologies are bringing the world's peoples and cultures closer together than at any time in human history. Today we need values that can deal with the moral subtleties that confront us in today's complex world.

But are our values up to this task? Or do we promote values that are too crude, too ideologically-driven, too judgmental, or too out-of-touch to work? Are our forebears' values still of value to us living in today's world? Are moral values eternal and unchanging? Or do values have a use-by date stamped into them? And the big question behind all these questions: How can we know?

This issue is significant today because we have politicians, religious leaders, economists, psychologists, militarists, social reformers, cultural commentators, legalists, and bloggers from all walks of life attempting to sell us very different ideas regarding what is right and wrong for us as individuals and collectively. Going to war, making money, punishing lawbreakers, pursuing terrorists, righting past colonial wrongs, exploiting the planet's natural resources, exploiting genetic technologies, addressing mass starvation and impoverishment—each of these issues raises complex moral questions. Many of us grapple with these complexities by trying to reduce what happens in the world to simple, easily comprehended formulas. But none of these questions is simple, none is easily comprehended, and none can be answered simply or easily.

We are each citizens, living in communities and cultures that accept particular moral values. But we are also individuals. As such, we are each responsible for our own decisions. So in order to become conscious moral beings the onus is on each of us to think through, for ourselves, what moral values we should live by. In this respect, being moral requires us to become introspective, because we need to decide what our values are before we can act on them.

Aristotle called human beings rational animals. Undeniably, our ability to think through problems and to find working solutions has led to the scientifically and technologically dominated environments we have made for ourselves. But rational thought also involves thinking abstractly. And abstract thought provides us with a way to travel across time, to project ourselves into the past and future, and to see what is not present—but that could be.

Our rationality has made it possible for us to create intricate networks of thought that allow us to consider what we are, to reflect on where we stand on the surface of this planet and in the vastness of the cosmos, and to prod and wonder at what we don't know. We can't help ourselves. Our very ability to think rationally, which is a function of our brain's cognitive capacities, compels us to investigate and speculate.

However, beyond Aristotle's definition of human beings as rational animals is our tendency to spiritualize. We think of ourselves as more than just another animal fighting for a place in the world, as more than merely the product of our environment, as more than an animal that lives for a few decades then vanishes into oblivion. No matter whether the urge is innate or a socialized response to our environment, over the millennia human beings have consistently demonstrated a compulsion to conceive of transcendent values that exist beyond our animal selves, values on which we develop into moral concepts.

Obviously, our need to moralize is intimately linked to the fact that we are social beings. We don't choose moral values in isolation; we choose them to better live with each other in the world. But our natural tendencies to rationalize and spiritualize underpin the way we moralize.

Rationality and morality are linked because it is only after weighing consequences that we decide whether an action is right or wrong. (If we respond automatically, without weighing consequences, it is because we apply the result of other people's reflections to the situation we face, i.e. we have let others do our thinking for us.)

Morality also reflects the idea that we should live in accordance with values that extend beyond the purely biological aspects of our existence. These values are intertwined with the spiritualization of our lives. Clearly, our spiritualizing tendency reflects the process of socialization, which gives us the feeling that we exist in spheres of activity that widen progressively from our body, to our family, to our community, to our nation, to our species, to our planet, to our solar system, and beyond. Yet these are spheres which we do not just occupy and exploit. They are also aspects of our lives towards which we consider we have a moral responsibility.

The ways we both spiritualize our feelings of social responsibility, and use rational thought to establish moral values, underpins this examination of morality. While many other aspects of our shared existence necessarily contribute to our sense of what morality is and how it impacts on our lives, this book focuses on the way we philosophize and spiritualize, and how we use them both to create the moral concepts and values that we apply in our lives.

Of course, counterbalancing this view of morality is the cold, hard reality of what we human beings actually do to each other. Human beings around the globe exhibit at best an unthinking disregard, and at worst a callous disdain, not just for their fellow human beings, but for all species of life. Indeed, many people use spirituality (in the form of religion), and rationalization (in the form of self and economic justification), as weapons with which to harm their fellow beings rather than progress our interlaced lives.

It is a commonplace that making a community and its citizens truly more moral, just, and "good" would stop much of this "bad" and its resulting suffering from occurring. Yet how can we achieve this goal? And, really, how many of us know what moral values all nations should adopt in order to *actually achieve* a more moral, just, and good world?

Some argue that making the world better is just a matter of establishing the right rules and paying enough law enforcement officers to ensure our fellow citizens adhere to them. Does this then mean that morality should consist of making lists of rules and not compromising on enforcing them? Others say morality is a matter of choice, and that each individual citizen should be free to make his or her own decision on what is good or bad. Where, then, should the moral criteria come from that we use to decide what is good or bad? From ourselves? From family? From social conventions? From conscience? From God?

This brings us to the question of what should be the basis of morality in today's world. Should we just live and let live? Or are there definite values that can help us define what truly is right and wrong?

These are all questions that are considered in this book. Because globalization is bringing all nations and cultures closer together, we urgently need to learn how to live peacefully, tolerantly, and justly with billions of our fellow human beings. In what follows I consider the ideas that underpin our assumptions about morality. I examine their development and how that has shaped our ideas about morality. I pay particular attention to morality in religious and historical contexts, balancing the idea of moral values as absolutes against relativist values and a developmental view of being moral.

My aim in what follows is to find a moral yardstick that is relevant to us today, living in the modern world, that we can use to guide us collectively into the future, as wiser, more tolerant, more compassionate, more spiritual, and more moral beings.

PART 1

THE GOOD LIFE

CHAPTER 1

Three Approaches To The Good Life

Morality, in its simplest sense, is the identification of what is good and bad in our lives. Being moral involves doing good rather than bad and living a good life. Being immoral means doing bad rather than good, and living an evil life. The idea that there is a morally good or evil life has an intriguing history.

The ancient Iranian prophet Zarathushtra, the founder of the Zoroastrian religion, who lived some time between 1400 and 1200 BCE in what is today north-eastern Iran, was the originator of the idea that human beings should be good in thought, word, and deed. He summed up his outlook in the *Gathas* (the poetic psalms he wrote), "Let all serve Ahura Mazda with words and deeds filled with good thought."[1]

The simple formula of "good thoughts, words, and deeds" permeates the prayers and writings of what Zarathushtra called the good religion. The Zoroastrian creed includes the promise, "I pledge myself to the well thought thought; I pledge myself to the well spoken word; I pledge myself to the well acted act," while a later hymn described Zarathushtra as "the first who thought what was good, the first who said what was good, the first who did what was good."[2]

Zarathushtra's people were tribal herdsmen who lived on the Central Asian steppes, driving their cattle across a huge expanse of grasslands under a seemingly limitless sky. This experience of the vastness of the world led the early Iranian herdsmen to conceive of God neither as a personalized being nor as a ruler or king (which is how the other religions of the era conceived of God), but instead as an abstract spiritual presence which transcends the world. The name Zarathushtra gave to God, Ahura Mazda, means Lord Wisdom. Zarathushtra viewed the good life as being one in which the just person follows the path of asha (asha means right, truth and order); cares for his or her inner self by cultivating good thoughts, words and deeds and by avoiding evil thoughts, words and deeds; is just with others; practices good husbandry in relation to cattle and plants; and offers worship to Ahura Mazda through ritual fire sacrifice, the fire being simultaneously a concrete manifestation and a symbol of asha. Through righteous worship, and by being open in thought, truthful in words, and kind in deeds, Zarathushtra considered that the just person would achieve happiness and fulfilment in this life and immortality in the next.

Openness, truthfulness, and kindness—these are "action" qualities that we can carry out in our lives. By presenting his concept of the good in this way, it is clear that Zarathushtra was not concerned with the good as an abstract concept, but rather with how the good might be integrated in a practical way into daily living. In his writings Zarathushtra offers no metaphysical, political, sociological, or economic arguments about the concept of goodness. Rather, he offers a way of living a good life.

Seven hundred years later, in Northern India, another influential contributor to human spirituality was born into what most of us would consider a very good life indeed. Siddhartha Gautama was a prince who was raised in palatial luxury. However, despite his protected life, he became troubled by the impact of suffering on human existence, particularly suffering created by illness, old age, and death. Legend says that, inspired by an ascetic monk, at the age of twenty-nine Siddhartha left his wife and new-born child, renounced his crown, moved to a forest, and began a series of extreme ascetic disciplines and practices in order to find spiritual enlightenment and a panacea to human suffering.

Siddhartha began by adopting the extreme ascetic practices of fasting and meditation advocated by the yogis of the day. But after a few years he rejected extreme bodily mortification and adopted a more moderate regime of practices that he later called the "middle way." This searching period of his life reached a climax in 528 BCE when he experienced a spiritual realization, after which he started teaching others how to achieve the wisdom he had achieved. Relevant to the notion of the good life is the teaching he called the Eightfold Noble Path.

Like Zarathushtra, the Buddha—as Siddhartha was now called—was not interested in defining good or goodness in the abstract. Instead, in the Eightfold Noble Path he created a practical framework for people to live by, in order to overcome suffering in their own lives and to achieve wisdom. The Buddha's Eightfold Noble Path, like Zarathushtra's path of asha, advocates right speech, right action, and right intention (which can also be translated as right thought) as a basis for living. However, to these three the Buddha added right livelihood, right perception, right effort, right mindfulness, and right concentration. Together, these eight qualities were designed not to create a new religion—the Buddha rejected both the Indian Brahmanic religion of his day and the very concept of God—but rather to provide a practical framework seekers could use to find wisdom for themselves. Thus the Eightfold Noble Path, like the Zoroastrian asha, presents the idea of the good life as a practical way of living morally with one's fellow human beings that simultaneously leads to spiritual wisdom.

However, the good life the Buddha envisaged differs from that of Zarathushtra. Where Zarathushtra lived on the Central Asian steppes, among tribesman who herded cattle for a living, the Buddha's thought was shaped by the Indian practice of renunciation. Thus the end goal as the Buddha conceived it was the state of nirvana, which literally means "extinguished." The state of nirvana is achieved when all those aspects burning inside us that feed the flame of suffering—such as fear, greed, hatred, and attachment to a desiring self—die away, leaving in their place an unconditioned experience of being alive in the world. Thus nirvana is the experience of being conscious and alive, but an experience emptied of desires and attachments which facilitates the flowering of a blissful state of being. Accordingly, while nirvana may be expressed in the negative terms of renunciation, it is actually a state of spiritual fullness and bliss that echoed Zarathushtra's concepts of wholeness and eternity.

Contemporary with the Buddha's India was another culture which was also thinking deeply about what humanity needs to achieve the good life—the Greeks. The Greek civilization extended from the coast of Anatolia (today's Turkey) in the East, across Greece, Italy and Sicily, to southern France in the West. Athens was the most populous and famous city-state in the Greek civilization. The Athenians were fascinated by the concept of the good. They wondered how people might live together harmoniously, and argued over what each individual's relationship to the city-state should be (debate was to Athenians what television is to us). Politically, this led to the development of the earliest known form of democracy. But central to all their debates was the question of what constituted the good life.

The Athenians considered that the good life manifested in the threefold pursuit of pleasure, honor, and knowledge. Pleasure entailed having a good time, honor meant being well thought of, and knowledge involved teaching the young the skills they needed to be good citizens. The social implications of this view are reflected in a popular Athenian song of the time:

> The very best thing for a person is health,
> Second good looks, and third honest wealth,
> The fourth to be in the prime of your life
> With people around you who do you no strife.[3]

But Athens was also the home of Greek philosophy. Around the same time that the Buddha began his teaching, Pythagoras is reputed to have invented the word philosophy, which means "love of wisdom." He set up the first philosophic communities, initially in his island home of Samos, then, after he was driven off by the island's tyrant ruler, in southern Italy. Philosophy for Pythagoras was not the academic philosophy taught in universities today. Rather, it was an attempt to understand the principles that lie hidden "within" our everyday existence.

Plato, Athens' greatest philosopher, lived from 427 to 347 BCE, approximately one hundred years after both Pythagoras and the Buddha. He combined Pythagoras' ideas with those of his teacher, Socrates, to develop a philisophic concept of the good life. In doing so, he turned the popular Athenian concept of the good life on its head. He started by dropping honor from consideration, on the grounds that pursuing a good reputation is of no worth to a philosopher. Instead, Plato considered the acquisition of knowledge to be the most worthy human pursuit. And he defined the pursuit of knowledge as consisting of living virtuously and seeking wisdom.

For Plato, philosophic wisdom consisted of knowledge of the Good. Plato also re-defined the role of pleasure in the good life, arguing that while sensual pleasure had its place (unlike the ancient Indians, the Greeks were not inclined towards asceticism), yet greater than sensual pleasure was the happiness derived from the acquisition of knowledge. Thus, as for Zarathushtra and the Buddha, Plato's concept of the good life was that it did not just involve living virtuously, but it also led to wisdom and happiness.

WHAT THE GOOD LIFE DOES NOT OFFER US

What these Zoroastrian, Buddhist, and Platonic concepts of the good life share is that they appeal to our highest ideals, they are humane and non-dogmatic, they are practical rather than theoretical, and even if we do not wish to practice them ourselves, we can see that they make sense. But there is one problem with them all. The problem is that these spiritual, moral, and humane qualities are not a snug fit with how we actually live today. In fact, they were not even a snug fit with how people lived in the times of Zarathushtra, Buddha, and Plato.

A graphic illustration of this is provided by an incident late in the Buddha's life. During his lifetime the Shakya clan he was born into had been making tributes to the nearby kingdom of Kosala. Then a new king came onto the throne of Kosala who decided he wanted the Shakya lands. So he had his soldiers capture all the Shakya clan's leaders. He then ordered them half-buried in the ground, and had a herd of elephants run over them. This action obliterated the Shakya clan's hereditary leadership.

Today the social model of success still centres on the acquisition of money, power, resources, and status. Competition between individuals, companies, corporations, and nations simmers at an confrontational level, ready at any time to develop into commercial, ideological, or physical warfare. While we have not had a world war for sixty years, throughout those years wars have continued to be fought, somewhere on the planet, every single day. So where does the ideal of a wisdom-fuelled good life fit into the messy human reality?

Plato considered this question in his book, *The Republic*. He argued that the only way to establish the good life in a society was either for kings to become philosophers, or for philosophers to become kings. The problem, of course, was that kings in those days (as with politicians today) were focussed on obtaining and holding onto power, and did not want to spend years studying philosophy. On the other hand, philosophers who developed wisdom were aware of the deadly games played by kings, the wealthy, and the powerful, and so they had no desire to enter politics.

Plato did, in fact, attempt to put his concept of a philosopher-king into practice after an old friend, Dion, persuaded him to teach philosophy to Dion's nephew, Dionysius II of Sicily, who had inherited the Sicilian throne at a young age. However, after several years the young king decided philosophy was not for him. So he banished Dion, and imprisoned Plato—twice. The first time Dionysius was persuaded to let Plato go, but the second time Plato only escaped death with the help of Pythagorean friends living in Southern Italy. (The Sicilians assassinated Dion a few years later, after he hired a mercenary army to invade Sicily so he could subjugate his own people.)

Plato eventually gave up the hope that humanity ever would adopt the philosophic good life. In *The Laws*, his last work, he went so far as to write what was, in effect, an elaborate list of do's and don'ts, ending up a kind of frustrated parent, his rules suggesting that if people can't make up their own minds to embrace the good life, then they'll just have to be told what's good for them!

THE PROBLEM WITH FINDING THE GOOD LIFE

Clearly, the messy reality is that there is much more to having the good flourish in our lives than merely laying out the principles of the good life, waiting for people to adopt them, and for all of us to reap the general happiness that inevitably follows. The world we have created for ourselves is too complex for such simple solutions—to the extent that it is tempting to agree with Solon, one of Greece's Seven Wise Men, that in reality none of us can truly be considered happy until we are dead.

Yet despite this most of us, no matter where we live, want to be happy. Overall we think of ourselves as good people who, on balance, try our best to make good decisions regarding what we do and how we live. And who among us doesn't want to make a good life for themselves, for their children, and for their grandchildren? I deliberately leave that question unanswered.

But how good are we really? Are the ideals we chase in today's world really taking us towards the good life? Or are they actually leading us away from it? Let's face it: if we are really good, and if our ideals truly are sound, why is the world we have created such a mess, and so filled with human-caused suffering?

Yet how should we define good and bad anyway? What criteria should we use to decide what behavior is acceptable and what is not? There are innumerable voices—political, religious, economic, social, military—telling us who are good and who are bad. What is the measure by which such judgments should most usefully be measured? How is it meaningful to claim that some of us are acting morally and some immorally? What is the practical moral yardstick we should use daily to decide, "This is good. This is bad"?

Finally, what about wisdom in relation to morality? Can the good really lead, as Zarathushtra, Buddha, and Plato claimed, to a whole, fulfilled, happy, and wisdom-filled life? Or is that just another daydream from the past? Is it even feasible today to make such an attempt? Can these ancient concepts of wisdom realistically fit into life as we live it today?

What follows, then, is a search for a moral yardstick.

What is required of this yardstick is that, firstly, it fits with how we life today in democratic, liberal, pluralist, free market societies; that, secondly, it offers an approach to morality that enables us to change ourselves, individually, and collectively, for the better; and that, thirdly, it accords with wisdom in a philosophic and spiritual sense.

The search begins in Part Two with a consideration of the social, political, and economic ideas regarding freedom and morality that have risen in the last three hundred years. A look back at key ideas from that period is necessary because what we think today has been shaped by thinkers from that time. And if we do not understand what they thought, and why, then we cannot properly appreciate how we came to shift from moral absolutism to moral relativism, which is the predominant form of morality we practice today.

Part Three critically examines social norms and customary practices, and considers how they have feed into our assumptions regarding what constitutes moral behavior.

Part Four considers concepts such as conscience and rewards and punishments in the afterlife, along with ideas propounded by a wide variety of religious, philosophic, and scientific thinkers with respect to them.

Part Five examines what contribution the concepts of the wisdom traditions can offer us in our search, particularly in relation to the exercise of conscience, the development of social and inner virtues, and the attainment of wisdom.

Finally, in Part Six, all the various threads are drawn together to offer a template for a moral yardstick that might conceivably work for us today.

PART 2

HOW SHOULD WE DEFINE THE GOOD?

CHAPTER 2

From Greek Ethics To "Show Me The Money!"

The search for a moral yardstick begins with a consideration of ethics. Ethics and morality are generally considered to be intertwined concepts, even interchangeable words. However, I will start by separating them, defining ethics as that part of morality that deals specifically with human interaction and behavior. I'll come back to morality, as such, later.

The word ethics has been derived both from the Greek word *ethos*, which means "character," and from *ethikos*, meaning "rising from habit." The Greeks considered that character was shaped by virtues. Indeed, virtues were so important to Plato that he argued that the growth of an individual's character was dependent on acquiring the four principal virtues of wisdom, courage, moderation, and justice. He also argued that the practice of these virtues was a prerequisite to living a happy and fulfilling life. Habit was significant because these virtues were best learnt through education, when the young could make them habitual behavior. For the Greeks in general, ethical virtues enabled individuals to make good decisions as citizens. For Plato, the philosophic point of acquiring the four virtues was that they led to the acquisition of wisdom.

Plato's ideas on the virtues were developed by his pupil, Aristotle, in his book, *Ethics*. Aristotle's writings had a huge impact on Christianity. Augustine of Hippo, the fourth century Church Father who was the first to develop a systematic Christian ethics, followed his mentor Ambrose of Milan in adapting the four Platonic and Aristotelian virtues of wisdom, courage, moderation, and justice into the four Christian cardinal virtues of temperance, fortitude, justice, and prudence.[1] For Augustine, temperance involved moderating sensual pleasures and appetites to reason, fortitude entailed practicing forbearance and courage, justice required regulating our actions in relation to others, and prudence necessitated practicing sagacity and wisdom.

Of course, the difference between Greek philosophy and Christian theology was that Plato and Aristotle saw the virtues as leading the philosopher towards widom, whereas the Church Fathers saw virtues as being performed in the service of God. Where the Greek philosophers considered human thought was the source for all moral codes—through all the ancient Greek world philosophers were regularly employed to formulate laws for cities—the Church Fathers saw God as the source of moral codes. And where the ancient Greeks saw moral codes as leading to being a good citizen, the Church Fathers saw virtues as leading to obedience of God.

The philosophic concepts of virtues proposed by Plato, expounded by Aristotle, and adopted by the Christian Church, and the idea that moral codes had their ultimate source in God, dominated Western culture until the seventeenth century, when they were first challenged by thinkers of the Ages of Reason and Enlightenment.

THE IMPACT OF RATIONALIST THINKING

The Ages of Reason and Enlightenment developed against the background of Europe's Thirty and Eighty Year Wars that ended in 1648 with the signing of

---

A COMPARISON OF ETHICAL FRAMEWORKS

PLATONIC ETHICS	AUGUSTINIAN ETHICS
• Four virtues: wisdom, courage, moderation, justice	• Four virtues: temperance, fortitude, prudence, justice
• The practice of virtues leads to wisdom and happiness	• The practice of virtues is an expression of service to God
• Moral codes are constructed using rational thought	• Moral codes are delivered to humanity by God
• Practicing moral codes is key to being a good citizen	• Practicing moral codes is key to obeying God's commands

FIGURE 2.1

the Peace of Westphalia. Historians today view this treaty as laying the political foundations for the modern era.

The Peace of Westphalia primarily promoted religious tolerance and established freedom of religious worship. But, politically, the treaty established the principles which still underpin international relations today: that states should have self-sovereignty and the right to political self-determination; that states should have equal legal status in international relations; and that no sovereign state should intervene in the internal affairs of another. The treaty also lifted trade barriers that had been erected during the wars.

The new freedoms of travel, commerce, and thought created a nurturing environment for a new wave of thinkers. Previously, Galileo Galilei, an Italian astronomer who died in 1642, had used observational science to confirm Copernicus' theory that the Earth circled the sun. The Catholic Church prevented Galileo from publishing his results, but the scientific method that underpinned his work was rapidly adopted by other thinkers. A key figure in this adoption was the English philosopher, Francis Bacon. He systematized the methodology of science, emphasizing the importance of experimentation, observation, and inductive reasoning. Bacon was followed by Descartes (whose "I think, therefore I am" is proverbial), and a host of other thinkers, including David Hume, John Locke, Thomas Hobbes, Immanuel Kant, Isaac Newton, Bishop Berkeley, Adam Smith, John Stuart Mill, and Thomas Paine.

Their shared practice of intellectual enquiry, and their acceptance of the validity of the scientific method, not only irrevocably changed the intellectual assumptions of Western culture, but was also grounded in a desire for social reformation. For centuries European nations had been ruled politically, economically, and morally by the twin institutions of the Christian Church and the hereditary aristocracy. Religion was stitched into the state's political structure. Royalty claimed they were anointed by God, and the aristocracy and clergy had linked interests which went back to the Middle Ages. The result was the social exploitation of the mases by an aristocratic and clerical few.

The eighteenth and nineteenth century thinkers responded to this situation by advocating for the establishment of a secular society, and by promoting rights for all individuals. As a result, over a period of two hundred years, from the late 1600s to the mid-1800s, the assumption that societies should be ruled by hereditary aristocrats was overthrown (a vehement argument which led to kingly and aristocratic heads rolling), the powers of Church and State were separated, democratically elected governments were created, and a profound reorganization of how Western nations were run politically and economically was effected. That all citizens should have political, social, religious, and intellectual freedom also became established as the social norm.

Obviously, too many individual thinkers and key ideas contributed to this transformation of Western culture to be dealt with here. So I will touch on just three thinkers from the post-Westphalian era whose ideas have impacted on contemporary ethical attitudes. These are the German philosopher Immanuel Kant, the Scottish philosopher and economist Adam Smith, and the English Utilitarian, John Stuart Mill.

IMMANUEL KANT

Immanuel Kant (1724-1804) was a towering genius of European thought. Kant was born into a strongly religious family who practiced a form of Lutherism. He remained a devout Christian throughout his life. Kant's writings are inarguably a difficult read. Nonetheless, a number of his ideas have impacted powerfully on Western intellectual culture. In particular, he questioned the basis of knowledge, asking how we can know anything at all. In his commitment to following through this line of line, he also questioned the validity of religiously-derived morality, metaphysical concepts, and the nature of our knowledge aquisition.

Kant studied the work of the mathematicans and scientists G.W. Leibniz and Isaac Newton at university, and wrote extensively on the sciences throughout his life. But it was in philosophy that he made his most significant contributions. He was appointed Professor of Metaphysics and Logic at Germany's University of Konigsberg in 1770, at the age of forty-five. His masterwork, *The Critique of Pure Reason*, was published in 1781. An 800 page monster, it was initially ignored. But in later decades, after others presented Kant's key ideas less impenetrably, the book came to be seen as a watershed in Western thought.

What separates Kant's ideas on morality from those of Plato and of the Church Fathers is that he argued for a moral principle that exists inside us, called the categorical imperative. Kant argued that moral codes do not exist outside us, as eternally ideal concepts, nor do they have their roots in divine revelation. Instead, he considered that each person was a morally autonomous being, and that we can each think through moral decisions for ourselves, using our innate powers of rational thought.

In his outlook Kant was a man of the Age of Enlightenment. It was assumed that all knowledge should be arrived at via rational thought. The Greek philosophers themselves had assumed this, as had Augustine and the Medieval Christian Scholastic theologians, led by Thomas Aquinas —although in the context of divine revelation. And two decades before Kant, the Scottish sceptic, David Hume, had argued, decisively for many (including Kant), that divine revelation was an inadequate source for knowledge of any kind.

What Kant did was to make an irrevocable break with the prevailing view that morality belonged in the realm of religion. Kant showed that morality has nothing to do with either religion or the divine revelation of moral codes. Instead, he argued, we are perfectly capable of deciding what is good or bad for ourselves, by thinking it through.

ADAM SMITH

Adam Smith was born in 1723 and died in 1790. A Scottish philosopher and economist, Smith is best known today as the first great advocate for the free market, in *An Enquiry into the Nature and Causes of the Wealth of Nations*, published in 1776, four years before Kant's *Critique*. Like Kant, Smith was influenced by the ideas of David Hume, with whom he formed part of the Scottish Enlightenment, a group of Scottish thinkers who contributed much to European politics, economics, and social philosophy.

One of Smith's most influential ideas is that what drives people is self-interest. He argued that the natural result of each person working to realize his or her own economic interests would be that the nation as a whole would also benefit, because as individuals became wealthier, the nations in which they live would also become wealthier. However, Smith's idea of self-interest was not identical with selfishness, because he also argued that self-interest should be mitigated by a sympathetic element:

> How selfish soever man may be supposed, there are evidently some principles in his nature, which interest him in the fortunes of others, and render their happiness necessary to him, though he derives nothing from it, except the pleasure of seeing it. Of this kind is pity or compassion, the emotion we feel for the misery of others, when we either see it, or are made to conceive it in a very lively manner.[2]

Smith argued that out of this natural sympathy for others comes a desire to see them benefit socially and economically. Thus our sympathy moderates our self-interest, ensuring we consider the interests of others along with our own.

Thus while Smith's ideas on the free market laid the ground for modern laissez-fair economics, at heart his concept of self-interest has little to do with the "dog-eat-dog" philosophy many in business adopt today.

JOHN STUART MILL

Like Adam Smith, John Stuart Mill was a philosopher and economist. Born in 1806, he was a gifted child, learning Greek at three, and reading Platonic dialogues in their original language by the age of eight. Along with mastering Latin and mathematics, he also studied the works of Aristotle, political economics, and the writings of Adam Smith.

Mill's father deliberately kept his son separate from other children during his early years. This separation, coupled with years of intense study, led Mill to have a breakdown at the age of twenty. He subsequently re-connected with his emotions through the writings of Wordsworth, whose poems helped him regain his psychological balance. As an adult Mill worked for a time for the British East India Company. He was also a Member of Parliament from 1865 to 1868, being the first person to advocate in Parliament for women to be given the vote.

What makes Mill significant with respect to ethics is his advocacy of Utilitarianism, a philosophic outlook that argues that an action's ethical value depends on its utility to the greatest number of people. Mill promoted this concept in a key work on social, political, and economic freedoms, *On Liberty* published in 1859, and in a highly influential essay, *Utilitarianism*, published in 1863.

Utilitarianism was actually first advocated by Jeremy Bentham, a philosopher and social reformer who was a close friend of Mill's father and was also Mill's godfather. Bentham agreed with the Greeks that ethical behavior would led to happiness. He developed "the greatest happiness principle", arguing that we can decide which public policies and personal actions are ethically right because they lead to the greatest happiness for the greatest number of people. Mill added to Bentham's ideas with his "harm principle" of freedom, arguing that we each should have the right to do whatever we want, as long as it doesn't harm others. Mill's "harm principle" is so deeply embedded in modern culture that it is difficult to understand how recent an idea of social interaction it actually is.

Mill and Bentham also had much to say about education. In Mills' day students at British universities were required to take orders in the Anglican Church before they could graduate. Despite his academic brilliance, because he didn't wish to take religious orders Mill refused to apply to either Cambridge or Oxford. In this respect, one of Jeremy Betham's initiatives was to advocate for the establishment of the University College London, admittance to which would be on a secular basis and open to all, whatever their class or background. Again, it can be seen that a idea that we regard as axiomatic to modern culture, that all cirizens should have access to education, not just the privileged few, is actually a very recent innovation.

While many other thinkers and social reformers contributed to the social, political and economic transformations that have shaped today's world, for our assumptions that each citizen has the right to act freely, to be educated, to vote, and to pursue personal happiness, we are undoubtedly indebted to the innovations of Mills and Bentham.

SECULAR ETHICAL FRAMEWORKS

IMMANUEL KANT

- We are independent moral agents
- Morality cannot be imposed on us from outside
- Moral codes are constructed using rational thought
- We make our own ethical decisions

ADAM SMITH

- We are independent moral agents
- Individuals are each driven by self-interest
- Sympathy for others mitigates our self-interest
- We consider others' interests along with our own

JEREMY BENTHAM

- We are individual moral agents
- Moral codes are constructed using rational thought
- Ethical behavior leads to the greatest happiness
- Ethical hinges on what is useful for attaining happiness

J.S. MILL

- We are iindependent moral agents
- Bentham's criteria of rational thought, happiness and utility
- We make our own ethical decisions independently
- Not harming others mitigates the actions we choose to undertake

FIGURE 2.2

THE ETHICAL RE-SHAPING OF THE WORLD

So we have three very significant sets of ideas. Kant proposed that each of us is an autonomous moral agent who is able to use rational thought to make moral decisions for ourselves, independent of external or traditional authorities. Adam Smith argued for a free market economy driven by sympathetic self-interest. And John Stuart Mill claimed that morality should be measured primarily in terms of social and personal goods, including freedoms, of access to education, and the right to live according to what makes us happy, as long we we don't harm others. Clearly, these are very recognizable features in today's social and moral landscape.

Ethically, these thinkers replaced the traditional Christian religious concept of good with various secular, humanist, social, political, and economic concepts. These included the idea that what was right or wrong should be derived rationally using a moral measure that exists within us (Kant); that we should be free from state controls in order to pursue our sympathetic self-interest (Smith); that the aim of ethics was to seek the greatest happiness for the greatest number of people (Bentham); and that we should be free to do anything we wished as long as our actions didn't harm others (Mill).

These are the ideas that underpin modern secular states. However, many people in the times of Kant, Smith, and Mill still believed in God, still attended church, and still had firm ideas regarding what was right or wrong. And even though we live today in secular states, many people contintue to advocate for the retention of traditional Catholic and Protestant ethical values.

CATHOLIC AND PROTESTANT ETHICS HANG ON

Where did Christian religiously-derived concepts of vices and virtues sit in relation to the new social concepts advocated by the post-Westphalian thinkers? Many answered this question either by maintaining their traditional religious virtues, or by adjusting their virtues so that they fitted better with the evolving secular states. These two lines of ethical thinking found expression in Catholic and Protestant ethics.

Over the centuries, Catholic theologicans developed a complex schema of virtues and vices. To the four Greek-inspired virtues of temperance, fortitude, justice, and prudence were added the theological virtues of faith, hope, and love. These seven became known as the cardinal or heavenly virtues. A lower level of virtues was then added. Known as the capital virtues, they consisted of humility, liberality, brotherly love, meekness, chastity, and diligence. Opposed to these virtues were the seven capital vices, popularly known as the seven deadly sins, of pride, greed, envy, wrath, lust, gluttony, and sloth. And below this level were yet more levels of mortal and venial sins.

Protestant virtues were not as systematized. Nor did they have an overtly religious perspective. Instead, they consisted of generalized attitudes about how we should live. While there was some overlap with Catholic virtues, in general Protestant virtues emphasized self-reliance—which is to be expected from an outlook that developed out of rejection of the Catholic Church and its religious values. Protestant virtues focused on those required to become a self-reliant individual. They included self-discipline, self-control, self-sacrifice (fulfilling duties to family and community), humility, and hard work. Protestant virtues coincided with the rise of capitalism, with which they fit admirably—"the Protestant work ethic" is still a phrase that is used today.

Catholic virtues and vices, grounded in the assumption that human beings are innately bad, soon lost their resonance in an inceasingly secular world. But by the late 1800s Protestant virtues had morphed into the Victorian virtues of hard work, thrift, temperance, fidelity, self-reliance, self-discipline, cleanliness, and godliness.[3] Accordingly, when people today decry the decline of virtues, and proclaim the need to punish more of a nation's "bad" cirtizens, they are usually thinking in the context of Protestant and Victorian virtues.

WHAT ETHICAL VALUES DO WE HAVE TODAY?

Given that modern culture is secular, liberal, democratic, pluralist, and market-driven, how relevant are the ethical values advocated by the Greeks and the Christian Fathers to our lives today?

Certainly, our values have little in common with the mono-cultural religious perspective of the Church Fathers. Their virtues have little influence on how we live, especially considering that we have institutionalized vices such as greed, gluttony, pride, and avarice into our lifestyles.

Plato's idea that happiness results from the acquisition of wisdom is far from today's view. Instead, the modern lifestyle agrees much more with the Greek idea that happiness hinges on having wealth and health, being surrounded by supportive family and friends, and looking good. We have also embraced the Greek idea that the good life hinges on pleasure, reputation, and being a good citizen—except we have tranformed the Greek appreciation of pleasure into consumerism, reputation has turned into an obsession with fame, and being a good citizen invoves being electronically plugged in.

Is this the future Kant, Smith, and Mill envisaged when they argued for the separation Church and State, and for the establishment of personal, political, intellectual, and economic freedoms? While these three were radicals in the way they changed how Europeans thought about themselves and their place in the world, personally they actually lived conservatively. None was a "me first" person in the way the concept of personal freedom is applied today. In general, they thought well of people and assumed not only that we all have the potential for good, but that given the opportunity we would all do good.

Similarly, while the modern world is money-dominated and consumer oriented, most of us would not agree that what we value most in our lives comes down to money, possessions, fame, and inter-connectivity. On the other hand, few of us would reject our modern lifestyle and embrace the good life of Plato's philosopher, or organize our daily activities to incorporate the Church Fathers' cardinal virtues.

Rather, most of us would likely say that we wish to embrace a middle way. We seek to make life better for ourselves and for our family, yet we remain sympathetic to the social and economic positions of others. We want freedom to pursue personal pleasure, but not necessarily at the expense of others' well-being. And, overall, we try to find a balance between fulfilling the economic, social, physical, creative, and personal goals we set ourselves, while also contributing in whatever way we can to the wider communities in which we live.

However, does this add up to an ethical existence? If so, of what kind? It is clear that there is no modern equivalent to the wisdom achieved by practicing Zarathushtra's path of asha, the Buddha's Eightfold Noble Path, or Plato's philosophic virtues. Instead the goals of modern secular nations largely focus on the acquiring of social and economic goods. This being the case, what ethical values should we adopt in order to decide what is good or bad?

Numerous thinkers have considered these questions, and have come up with a range of fascinating suggestions. So an examination of what has been thought in the past can only help clarify our thinking about what is required today. The starting point is an acknowledgement of the huge cultural gulf that separates us from our forebears, a gap that is responsible for the very different ways we think about everything today.

MORAL OBJECTIVISM VS MORAL RELATIVISM

A key contributor to the creation of the gulf that exists between our forebears' views on morality and what we think today is the shift from moral objectivism to moral relativism. Moral objectivism is the view that there is a clear criteria by which we can judge right and wrong, and that that moral criteria exists outside and beyond our personal perspective. Those who argue that God has given us a moral code are moral objectivists. In contrast, moral relativism is the view that there is no absolute right and wrong, that each society has the right to decide for itself what it considers to be right and wrong, and that each society's moral outlook is equally valid.

As Western nations cast off their feudal hierarchies—in which the clergy morally stood over the community, the Church morally stood over the clergy, and God morally stood over the Church—they also threw off the traditional moral certainties their Churches provided. Subsequently, as modern nations became more pluralist in their political and social structures, a multiplicity of moral perspectives grew, to the extent that there has inevitably risen the view

A COMPARISON OF MORAL OUTLOOKS

MORAL OBJECTIVISM	MORAL RELATIVISM
• Moral values and goals are centred on a universal absolute, ie. God, or some transcendent idea	• Moral values and goals have no universal or absolute source, being culturally generated
• Values are universally valid, so generate absolute rights and wrongs	• Values are culturally dependent, so there are no absolute rights and wrongs
• There exist clearly defined virtues that are used to achieve absolute religiously generated social goods	• There exist culturally agreed virtues that are used to achieve socially agreed and therefore relative social goods

FIGURE 2.3

that everything in life today is relative. So overall we have ditched the absolute concepts of right and wrong that Christianity previously provided in favor of relativist ethical values.

In the next two chapters I will use these categories of moral objectivism and moral relativism to examine in more detail the key perspectives that have shaped modern attitudes towards ethics. I won't go into all the intricacies of argument that academy philosophers employ in relation to these perspectives. As a result, what follows will inevitably contain a number of over-simplifications. But the pay-off is it will enable us to obtain an overview of a range of significant ethical positions. I'll start by examining the development of the moral relativist view.

CHAPTER 3

Good And Bad:
Is It All Relative?

The thinkers of the eighteenth and nineteenth centuries advocated concepts that resulted in the shift of the Western ethical outlook from Christian moral absolutism to secular moral relativism.

The key implications of moral relativism, which most of us accept today, are that we each should have the right to choose how we live our lives (as long as we don't harm others); that we don't have a right to dictate how others should live (even if it's not how we might want to live); that upbringing and environmental impact on people, causing them to act harmfully towards themselves or others (some upbringings are better than others); and that there aren't really any moral absolutes in the world, there is only what we decide within the context of where we live (what is right for me may not be right for you, and visa versa).

This doesn't mean that Westerners go out each night stealing and plundering. Clearly, most of us don't. But in general terms this shift has lead to a liberal, secular, and (reasonably) accepting moral outlook that could be characterized as, "We're all in this world together, so let's make the best of it."

How did this cultural turn-around of perspective from certainty to relativism come about? How did we shift from a clear ethical understanding of how we should behave to the cacophony of voices that today argue about the role and purpose of ethics, culture, politics, religion, economics, gender, and art in our lives?

One answer is that a significant shift occurred in the period after the end of World War Two, and particularly during the period from the late 1950s to the mid-1970s, when a new prosperity stimulated considerable social changes. Prosperity changed the lives of women, developed a new youth culture, and stimulated the migration of millions from poor underdeveloped countries to the wealthier developed world.

In the 1950s the middle classes became wealthier and parents sought to give their children the opportunities they hadn't had during the austerity of the preceding war years. This led to the creation of a new social category of teenagers. Although teenagers are popularly associated with the rise of rock music, they became cemented by the cultural and advertising industries who saw opportunities to sell products to this new youth market. Another key aspect was the new economic and sexual freedoms, which enabled women to escape complete dependency on men and to forge their own careers and lives outside a social structure centred on family and making babies. And the promise of plentiful work stimulated the migration of millions into Western nations, often to the countries who had previously colonized them, where work, education, and higher standards of living were available.

Over forty years later, conservative members of Western societies still have issues with the resulting sexual freedoms, social freedoms, economic freedoms, and the multiple cultural perspectives that developed post World War Two, but that are now embedded in our world. Yet, as was shown in the previous chapter, these changes actually go much further back in time. So I will now look back again and examine how relativist views came to dominate Western culture.

THE SHIFT FROM CERTAINTY TO RELATIVISM

During the Post-Enlightenment era discussed in the previous chapter, European colonialism also reached its height. Great Britain, France, Portugal, Netherlands, and Spain each ruled colonies in Africa, Asia, South America and the Pacific, maintaining extensive networks of European economic and cultural influence that stretched around the globe. Such networks transmitted some of the fruits of industrialization and modernization from Europe to their colonies. However, Europeans also tended to be persuaded of their cultural, intellectual, and moral superiority. This led many colonial rulers to exploit, judge, or attempt to correct what they viewed as the ignorance, inferiority, irreligiousness, and immorality of their colonized charges.

After World War Two most colonized counties achieved independence. The internationalism promoted by the United Nations also extended the Treaty of Westphalia into the global arena, advocating that all states should have the right to political self-determination, equal legal status in international relations, and that one sovereign state should not intervene in the internal affairs of another.

Thus European nations were required to treat their former colonies, and all other countries in the same region, as equals. As a result, the previously unthinkingly accepted belief in European Christian values as absolute started to dissipate, and relativist modes of thinking began to be adopted.

Moral relativism, as it is understood today, has also been strongly shaped by anthropology and ethnography. Victorian explorers and researchers largely viewed non-European cultures through a lens tinted by their own assumed superiority, as is discernible in terms such as "savages," "heathens," "uncivilized brutes," that are common in Victorian-era literature. By the mid-twentieth century anthropologists and ethnographers had adopted a non-judgmental, scientific attitude, which led them to accept that the ethical values people lived by were perfectly valid within the parameters of their own culture. Concepts of right and wrong were now seen to be cultural constructs rather than moral absolutes. In 1947, "on the occasion of the United Nations debate about universal human rights, the American Anthropological Association issued a statement declaring that moral values are relative to cultures and that there is no way of showing that the values of one culture are better than those of another."[4]

This shift to a relativist outlook is reflected in the way today's university-centred philosophers tend to think about ethics. Academic philosophy divides ethics into three areas: normative ethics, meta-ethics, and applied ethics. Normative ethics examines social norms of conduct (what we, as a culture, agree is normal and acceptable behavior); meta-ethics investigates the nature of statements made about ethical issues, focussing in particular on the logic and language that are involved when we ask questions about ethics; and applied ethics deals with practical spheres such as legal ethics, medical ethics, and biotech ethics, and also with how normative ethics work in societies today in relation to issues such as the death penalty, going to war, or abortion.

Those thinking within these three categories today are largely agreed that ethical judgments are relativist phenomena, and that there exist no indisputable absolute or objective criteria for making moral statements and judgments. Thus the meta-ethical position on moral relativism is that, "the truth or falsity of mortal judgments, or their justification, is not absolute or universal, but is relative to the traditions, convictions, or practices of a group of persons."[5]

Such a shift to relativism was not unprecedented. In ancient Athens, Protagoras, one of the greatest of the Sophists (teachers of rhetoric and virtue), wrote in his one book, modestly titled *The Truth*, "Man is the measure of all things."

Plato observed that Protagoras himself explained this statement as meaning, "Each and every event is for me as it appears to me, and is for you as it appears to you—you and I being 'man."[6] That is, Protagoras argued that each human being has his or her own subjective perception of the world, which is real and valid for that person. Relativism has deep roots in Western culture.

An interesting implication of moral relativism is the way that it leads to moral subjectivism. Moral relativism is based on the perception that different cultures, which live according to different social norms, have their own ideas regarding what is ethically good or bad. Having accepted this, the next step is to accept the validity of differences in ethical perspectives not just between whole societies, but also between different groups within each of those societies, then between individuals in each group. So we end up adopting the view that each individual may validly adopt and practice their own personal ethical values.

This is moral subjectivism, which rejects the idea that there should be universal social norms in favor of the idea that each citizen has the moral right to decide for him or herself what ethical values to live by, independent of those they live with. Teenagers make a crude case for this perspective when they tell their parents, "You're not the boss of me," i.e. "I can do what I want." The English Satanist, Alistair Crowley, advocated much the same position when he claimed "Do what thou wilt" should be the only law that applies to individuals.

A more considered advocacy of the subjectivist position is offered by libertarianism, which argues that the many state controls that place limits on the activities of individuals are not morally valid because they repress the individual who has the right to think, do, and say as he or she wishes. In economic terms, libertarians consider that the state's forcing of individuals to pay taxes is illegitimate, as is the whole concept of the welfare state.

But how pragmatic is it really to allow everyone in a society to adopt a fully subjectivist ethical position? If there are no clear and agreed values in place, won't this just lead to social anarchy? Isn't a society justified in requiring its citizens to conform to socially agreed limitations on their behavior? John Stuart Mill offered answers to these questions in his advocacy of liberalism.

LIBERALISM

While there is at least a little "I want to do what I want to do" in each of us, as citizens living with other citizens we do not expect to be able to do everything we want. Nor do we expect others to be able to do all they want either. The vast majority of us accept that we should live according to rules that regulate our interactions with each other. But once Western societies dismantled the previous religiously-oriented moral structure, derived jointly from the Bible and fuedally-derived social norms, where would ethical rules come from?

Both Bentham and Mill foresaw the implications of dismantling the traditional value systems offered by Church and aristocracy. Bentham deliberated at depth how laws might be justly formulated to promote the greatest happiness for the greatest number of people. Mill made an equal contribution to promoting individual freedoms by developing the concept of liberalism, which he introduced in *On Liberty* (1859). He earlier worked through the implications of this position in *Principles of Political Economy* (1848).

What Mill advocated in liberalism was the concept of liberty as fundamental to a society's political, economic, and legal processes. He laid the foundations for contemporary Western liberal democracies by advocating equal rights for all, freedom of conscience, the establishment of a market economy, and endorsing private enterprise and individual property and contractual rights for governing economic relations. He also argued that government should be transparent, and that limitations should be placed on the rights governments had to control their citizens. Liberal democracy had become the form of government of all Western countries by the late 1880s—indeed, the USA broke away from British rule in the name of "life, liberty, and the pursuit of happiness," and included the aims of liberalism in its Bill of Rights.

However, as has been previously observed, we don't have complete freedom, because balancing the freeing impulses of liberalism are the limiting factors of the law. To maintain a degree of social order acceptable to the majority, and in particular to stop "bad" citizens harming "good" citizens, all nations have established laws that place limits on its citizens' actions, so they do not have the freedom to do absolutely anything they want. But, of course, this brings us back to Mill's concern that governments should not overstep the mark in the laws they generate.

An example of this tension between individual rights and the need for wider social control is provided by the anti-terror laws that many Western countries have passed in the wake of the 9-11 attacks in the USA. These laws restricted citizens' travel, speech, and assembly. But such legislation also diminishes the package of hard-won freedoms that provide the foundations of liberal democracies. This has given rise to considerable debate over what should be the proper balance between a citizen's freedom on the one hand, and the state's right to control citizen's activities in order to protect the wider populace on the other.

SUMMARY

So where has all this taken us? On the one hand, we live in liberal democracies, within an intellectual climate dominated by relativist thinking, in which absolutist Greek philosophic and Christian virtues and values have been replaced as a result of social and economic changes. On the other hand, we need social norms and ethical rules to hold a society together, a requirement which is acknowledged in the way people accept that living harmoniously with others involves trade-offs between what individuals want and what is best for all citizens collectively.

A number of clear pluses rise from the moral relativist view, as do a number of minuses. For example, it is a major plus that we have greater freedom to think, do, and say what we wish, than was afforded our forebears; but it is a minus that we lack our forebears' moral certainties. A plus is that we have the rule of law to set standards of social behavior, to moderate our treatment of one another, and to provide a degree of ethical certainty; a minus is that all laws are relativist constructs that by their nature cannot provide any ultimate test for what is truly right or wrong—and the wealthy have an advantage over the less wealthy in the degree to which they can utilize the process of the law, which is an expensive process. A plus is that other people are not telling us all the time what is right or wrong, resulting in our each having the opportunity to decide for ourselves what we think is ultimately right or wrong; a minus is that in a relativist world is it even sensible to think there could be an ultimate moral yardstick?

Possible answers to these questions are offered by the outlook called moral objectivism.

CHAPTER 4

Is There A Definite Moral Yardstick?

Moral objectivism is based on the view that there is an objective moral yardstick, existing seperate from us personally, which can be used to decide whether people's actions are good.

As noted earlier, religions such as Judaism, Christianity, and Islam offer frameworks of moral objectivism that are considered to emanate from God. However, moral objectivism also exists outside a religious context. Examples include the philosophies of Plato, who believed in the Good as the ultimate moral goal; of Kant, who argued for human reason as the ultimate arbitrator on moral issues; and of Utilitarians such as Bentham and Mill who considered that the goal of universal happiness provided an objective yardstick by which we should measure moral goods and moral progress. Academic philosophers name these the rationalist category of moral objectivism. In addition, there is also the rationalist religious category which Thomas Aquinas developed.

To structure this chapter, I will use these three religious, rationalist, and rationalist religious categories of moral objectivism. (See FIGURE 4.1)

THE RELIGIOUS CATEGORY

The religious category of moral objectivism is applied by believers who accept the existence of a personal God, and who consider God has given humanity moral guidance through revelation. This revelation has come via the proclamations of prophets or through holy scriptures such as the Judaic Ten Commandments, the Christian *Sermon on the Mount*, Islam's *Qur'an*, and the Hindu *Manu Smriti*. Religious moral objectivists argue that God's revelation provides an absolute moral yardstick for measuring which human actions are good and which bad.

Religious moral objectivism places God at the pinnacle of human existence. Choosing between good and bad actions is done on the basis that good actions are those that are in harmony with God's commands, while bad actions depart from God's commands. Of course, there is the question as to whether religious moral dictums are generated by God, or are instead social constructs that have later been given authority by called said to be given by God. I'll come back to this issue later.

One concept of Christian moral objectivism that has had a huge impact on Western culture is original sin. According to this idea, humanity is born sinful and so is in permanent need of moral redemption. As the Catechism of the Catholic Church states:

> By his sin Adam, as the first man, lost the original holiness and justice he had received from God, not only for himself but for all human beings. Adam and Eve transmitted to their descendants human nature wounded by their own first sin and hence deprived of original holiness and justice; this deprivation is called 'original sin'. As a result of original sin, human nature is weakened in its powers, subject to ignorance, suffering and the domination of death, and inclined to sin.[7]

THE THREE CATEGORIES OF MORAL OBJECTIVISM

RELIGIOUS	RATIONALIST	RELIGIOUS RATIONALIST
• God gives us our moral code via religious revelation	• We arrive at moral codes using our ability to think rationally	• God's revealed moral code can be understood using reason
• Good occurs when we obey God's code	• Good occurs when we act according to our ideal	• Good occurs when we obey God's code
• Bad occurs when we disobey God's code	• Bad occurs when we depart from our ideal	• Bad occurs when we disobey God's code
• God's commands are rmoral absolutes	• Moral ideals are independent of individuals	• God's commands are religious absolutes

FIGURE 4.1

The assumption that humanity's natural moral state is one of sinfulness has had a powerful psychological impact on Western cultures, generating negative attitudes such as guilt and worthlessness. It is interesting to consider whether the English secular legal system, which assumes that the accused is innocent rather than guilty was created as a reaction to Christian morality—which assumes that all human beings are born guilty. The impact that the concept of original sin has had on the Western outlook is so important that it requires further thought. Accordingly, I will return to it more fully later. For now I'll move on to consider the rationalist category.

THE RATIONALIST CATEGORY

The rationalist approach to defining morality rejects God's revelation as the source of moral codes. Instead, it considers that by engaging in reasoned thinking we can arrive at an objective framework for deciding which of our actions are right and which wrong.

Plato considered perception of the Good is the pinnacle of human existence. Like the Christian Fathers, he thought that living a good life took us towards the Good, while not doing so took us in the other direction. Plato argued that various moral goods enable us to live the good life, that these goods exist separate from us, in the intelligible realm, and that they can be accessed in that realm by rational thought. Thus the moral norms by which we should live exist as ideal objective concepts that transcend subjective human existence.

Kant sought a universal objective moral standard in what he termed the categorical imperative. He considered the categorical imperative gave us a moral standard that applied equally to everyone, whatever their race, nationality, religion or cultural background; that would enable us to rise above subjective concepts of right and wrong; and that it offers us a way of deciding what is morally correct in all circumstances. As with Plato's moral goods, the categorical imperative is arrived at through practicing rational thought. From it, Kant derived a number of formulations regarding moral actions. In deriving these formulations, he assumed that human beings are rational, have free will (which, in a clear rejection of the concept of original sin, is fundamentally rational and good, not irrational and bad), and are able to act as independent moral agents. This led to his first three formulations being:

1: Act only according to that maxim by which you can at the same time will that it would become a universal law. 2: Act in such a way that you always treat humanity, whether in your own person or in the person of any other, never simply as a means, but always at the same time as an end. 3: So act as though you were through your maxims a law-making member of a kingdom of ends.

In the first formulation, Kant sought a way to universalize our moral behavior by asking: Would we be happy if the action we were about to undertake became a universal law? For example, if we were in a supermarket, and had just secured from another shopper a trolley to shop with, would we be happy for it become a universal law that everyone could take anyone else's shopping trolley whenever they needed one? This would mean that the trolley we were using could be taken by another shopper in the middle of our own shopping.

In his second and third formulations Kant drew on the widespread eighteenth century idea of duty to declare that we have an obligation to others. To Kant, this meant that any action we must not be performed to use others as a means for us to achieve our personal ends. Other people are rational, free-willing, morally autonomous beings—just like us—who have the moral right to carry out their own actions. So in our actions we should not treat others as a means to achieve our goals. If this sounds familiar, it is, as some critics argue that Kant's categorical imperative is really only a philosophized version of the Golden Rule, which states that we should treat others as we would be treated ourselves.

The way these three formulations operate practically can be seen in how Kant considered deceitful, deceiving, and murderous actions to be immoral because in carrying them out we treat others as a means to achieve our ends, ignoring the fact that their ends would not involve themselves being deceived, lied to, or murdered. Further, if we derived universal laws from our actions, everyone would be required to deceive, lie and murder all the time. Obviously, this is not a good idea, not just because it would make life awkward, but because it prevents other human beings from functioning as rationally functioning independent moral agents.

A third example of the rational category of moral objectivism is provided by Utilitarianism. Mill adopted Bentham's Greatest Happiness Principle which states that morality should provide the greatest happiness to the greatest number. However, while he accepted Betham's criteria of utility, Mill extended it by arguing that the happiness that results "is not the agent's own greatest happiness, but the greatest amount of happiness altogether."[8]

Two significant concepts were later derived from Mill's position. The first is consequentialism, which considers that the moral value of actions should be decided on the basis of their consequences. Thus it doesn't matter what people intend to do, or what the motives behind their actions are. All that really matters ethically is what occurs as a result of our actions. The second is Utilitarianism's universalizing tendency, this being that the most moral action should have the best consequences for as many people as possible, and not just the best consequences for the individual who carries out that action.

There are many different interpretations and applications of Utilitarian ethics today. For example, Utilitarian thinkers variously offer the universal goals of individual liberty, social justice, material equality, hedonistic pleasure, and political freedom as ethical goals alternative to Bentham's Greatest Happiness Principle. There are too many positions to survey here, so I'll focus on just one, that of ethical philosopher, Peter Singer. Singer states as his position that:

> An ethical principle cannot be defended in relation to any partial or sectional view. Ethics takes a universal point of view. This does not mean that a particular ethical judgment must be universally applicable. ... What it does mean is that in making ethical judgments we go beyond our own likes and dislikes. From an ethical point of view, the fact that it is I who benefits from, say, a more equal distribution of income and you who lose by it, is irrelevant. Ethics requires us to go beyond 'I' and 'you' to the universal law, the universalizerable judgment, the standpoint of the impartial spectator or ideal observer.[9]

Singer opens up the idea of consequences, replacing Mill's concept that the most ethical actions create the greatest happiness with an even broader concept of universalized interests. He argues that when we consider an action's ethical consequences, we should consider the interests of all those affected. So when we build a public park, some may want their housing not to be affected, some may be concerned about gangs congregating in the park, others may want more car parking spaces, and officials require legal requirements be satisfied. Singer's best consequences perspective is that the most ethical decision in this situation will be the one that best satisfies all the parties involved.

Clearly, Singer assumes that rational thought is necessary to deciding how to act ethically. Equally clearly, he also embraces Kant's universalizing tendency. The strength of Singer's position—he calls it a minimalist way of "universalizing self-interested decision-making"[10]—is that he has developed it as a process for achieving ethical decision-making for those living in secular, liberal, pluralist cultures, where it is necessary to take into account multiple perspectives, and not to measure decisions against an absolute moral yardstick.

A fourth example of the rationalist approach to moral objectivism is provided by objectivist ethics, which were conceived by the late twentieth century writer and philosopher of economics, Ayn Rand. Rand built on the idea of self-interest as advocated by Adam Smith. Rand accepted many of the ideas we have been discussing, including the premise that we are rational animals, that the goal of human existence is happiness, Kant's idea that we are morally autonomous beings, and Bentham's assumption that bodily pleasure and pain are the criteria by which we should measure happiness.

However, where Rand differs from these thinkers is that she does not accept general happiness as humanity's ultimate moral goal. Rather, she makes the individual's happiness the pinnacle of human existence. For Rand, an individual "must exist for his own sake, neither sacrificing himself to others nor sacrificing others to himself. The pursuit of his own rational self-interest and of his own happiness is the highest moral purpose of his life . . . My philosophy, in essence, is the concept of man as a heroic being, with his own happiness as the moral purpose of his life, with productive achievement as his noblest activity, and reason as his only absolute."[11]

Rand derived a number of implications from this view. Rejecting Kant's eigtheenth century idea of social duty, she argued that duty is immoral because its obligations come from outside us, and so inhibit our individual freedom and our ability to fulfil our personal life goals. She argued further that the only obligations we should have are those that we voluntarily choose for ourselves, that the good in our lives only exists in relation to the goals we set ourselves, that the values that enable us to select goals are reason, purpose, and self-esteem, and that the virtues which enable us to apply these good values are rationality, productiveness, and pride. By using rational thought, we develop life goals to focus our productivity. Productivity gives our life purpose, and we can rightfully be proud when we achieve our life goals.

Rand was against violence between states and individuals on the grounds that it is irrational, and it is not in our interest to disrupt the market mechanisms by which trade and business are carried out. Clearly, Rand's reshaping of rationalist self-interest into objectivist ethics offers an interesting philosophic view for living in Western materialist, late-capitalist societies.

The final example of a rational objectivist moral approach is that offered by the new Darwinists. Evolutionary theory, as espoused by Richard Dawkins, Steven Pinker, and Daniel Dennett, argues that our genes should be thought of as the objective yardstick by which the ethical quality of our actions can be measured.[12] According to this theory, our physical body is a gene-carrying vehicle. Genes have an automatic, blind, unconscious, and ruthless intent to survive and replicate themselves. This means that all humanity's diverse social, cultural, economic, and ethical behavior can be explained as a manifestation of our gene's innate urge to survive by adapting the vehicle of their body to the environment, then to use their vehicle to reproduce. The most successful genes are the ones that best adapt and survive. They become the fittest:

> Natural selection is an inanimate process, devoid of consciousness, yet is a tireless refiner, an ingenious craftsman. … Darwin once summed up natural selection in the words: "Multiply, vary, let the strongest live and the weakest die." Here "strongest," as he well knew, means not just brawniest, but best adapted to the environment, whether through camouflage, cleverness, or anything else that aids survival and reproduction. The word fittest (a coinage Darwin didn't make but did accept) is typically used in place of strongest, signifying this broader conception—an organism's "fitness" to the task of transmitting its genes to the next generation, within its particular environment. "Fitness" is the thing that natural selection, in continually redesigning species, perpetually "seeks" to maximize. Fitness is what made us what we are today.[13]

Neo-evolutionary theorists have identified a number of strategies that genes have developed to survive and reproduce. The first is kin selection. We care more for family and relatives than for strangers because if our body dies at least those genes we share with family and relatives will survive.

A second strategy is familial and sibling love. This occurs because genes incline "human beings to sense early on who their siblings are and thereafter share food with them, give guidance to them, defend them, and so on—genes, in other words, leading to sympathy, empathy, compassion: genes for love."[14] Hence genes' strategy of kin selection leads us to express love.

A third strategy is reciprocal altruism. Our genes drive us to help others to survive, because we may need their help in the future. Hence reciprocal altruism leads us to give now, and to seek nothing in exchange. But we are gambling that it will buy us help when we need it in the future.

With reciprocal altruism goes the fourth strategy, that of punishing cheaters. We have to punish those who do not reciprocate acts of altruism. Punishment has various degrees, from projecting guilt and shame onto those who cheat, to banishment, or death. Thus, over time, the genes of cheaters have been weeded out of the gene pool.

A fifth strategy is the development of conscience, which is viewed entirely as a strategy for adaptation and survival. In order to survive in any environment,

SIX TYPES OF RATIONAL MORAL OBJECTIVISM

PLATO

- Moral aim: To attain to the transcendent Good
- We attain to the Good by living the good life
- We live the good life by practising moral goods
- We identify moral goods using rational thought

KANT

- Moral aim: To act as an independent moral agent
- Achieved by universaling moral decision-making
- Live by treating others as free moral agents
- We make moral decisions using rational thought

MILL

- Moral aim: To create the greatest happiness
- The greatest happiness should be for everyone
- Live aiming to achieve the best consequences
- These consequences should be best for everyone

SINGER

- Moral aim: To universal-ize self-interest
- Set aside personal likes and dislikes
- Live by considering the interests of all involved
- Use rational thought to decide on a universalized course of action

RAND

- Moral aim: To create happiness for oneself
- Consider self-interest the most important interest
- Live to achieve personal productive fulfillment
- Use rational thought to decide on the best course of personal moral action

NEO-DARWINISTS

- Moral aim: There is no fundamental moral aim
- Instead our genes seek to survive and reproduce
- The genes' survival and reproduction give rise to behavioral strategies
- These strategies create what we call morality

FIGURE 4.2

human beings have to cooperate with others in order to survival. For example, if there is a shortage of food or water, our genes don't want other genes cheating and getting more than their fair share, because this will diminish our genes' ability to survive. So to control other's behavior we have developed such emotions as moral outrage, indignation, and a tendency to judge. Conscience is the combined drive of these strageies.

In all this, it is the activities of what Richard Dawkins famously called "selfish genes" that have given rise to higher moral functions such as love and altruism, which are generated by genes striving to survive and replicate, genes for which we human beings are no more than vehicles. From the neo-evolutionary perspective there is no set moral code, just an innate urge in human beings to behave morally—in their genes' self-interest. As Robert Wright explains:

> A moral code is an informal compromise among competing spheres of genetic self-interest, each acting to mould the code to its own ends, using any levers at its disposal. ... Though there's nothing inherently good about genetic self-interest, there's nothing inherently wrong with it either. When it does conduce to happiness (which it won't always), and doesn't gravely hurt anyone else, why fight it? ... Few evolutionary psychologists would quarrel with Daly and Wilson's basic view that "Morality is the device of an animal of exceptional cognitive complexity, pursuing its interests in an exceptionally complex social universe."[15]

Interestingly, of the five types of rational moral objectivism I have examined, only evolutionary theory is both reductionist and absolutist in its outlook, because it considers that the biological urge emanating from genes' need to survive and replicate provides a complete explanation for all life, to which nothing else needs to be added. Only religion provides an equivalent, although very different, absolutist outlook. Perhaps one reason many people feel uncomfortable with evolutionary theory is that we live in an era in which people making absolutist claims, whether religious, political, economic, or biological, have tended to create a lot of misery for other people.

Nonetheless, Neo-Darwinism has thrown up some interesting ideas with regard to morality, to which I will return in Chapter Ten.

THE RATIONAL RELIGIOUS CATEGORY

The rational religious position argues that while God offers humanity a moral code via revelation, that code is also available to us through rational thought. This is because God designed the universe with his intellect, which we can access by using our own intellects. This position was first argued by Thomas Aquinas in an attempt to reconcile revelatory Christian theology with the rationalist philosophy of Aristotle and Plato.

But Aristotle was a Greek philosopher and Aquinas a Christian theologian. So where Aristotle considered wisdom to be the ultimate goal, Aquinas considered the ultimate goal to be *felicitas*, the uninterrupted vision of God. In its fullest expression this could only be achieved in the afterlife. However, something of it could be attained in this life by using rational thought to comprehend the world. Aquinas also considered that developing an understanding of the natural laws that governed the world enabled believers to understand the mind of God. And developing practical reasoning could lead believers to pragmatic, ethical, and religiously sound solutions regarding how to act in the world.

Aquinas' first moral principle was that we have free will. We can choose how to act. The activity of choosing requires the use of practical reason, the first principle of which is, "good is to be done and pursued, and evil is to be avoided". Good or evil are part of the world's natural laws. And we use practical reason to comprehend and apply those those laws.

From the first principle of free will Aquinas then derived three further goods: to preserve our life, to marry and raise children, and to come to rationally know the truth about God and the right way to live with others.[16] Ethical actions were thus rational and intelligible, because they are derived from the first principle of practical reason and its three associated goods.

Aquinas also considered, with the Greeks, that practicing moral virtues helps us refine our moral character. However, where Aquinas' position differed was that he considered love, rather than wisdom, should be humanity's principal guiding ethical principle. And, as has already been noted, acting virtuously ultimately takes believers towards *felicitas*.

TRANSCENDENCE AS THE GOAL OF MORALITY

In contrast to Aquinas, the moral goals of Kant, Mill, Singer, Rand, and the

Neo-Darwinists are clearly in this world. Whether decisions are made by rationalizing the way we treat others, by taking into consideration what leads to the greatest happiness for the greatest number of people, by universalling self-interested decision-making, by focusing on personal goals, or by our genes manipulating our behavior in order to survive and reproduce, the decisions made all have a moral goal that is firmly grounded in the world of our everyday existence. In contrast, Aquinas' concept of *feliitas* as a moral goal means that while our actions are performed in this world, the ultimate aim of acting morally is not in this world but in a transcendent spiritual realm.

The idea of a transcendent otherworldly moral goal is explicit in all religions, whether it is expressed in terms of living for eternity in a heavenly or hellish realm, or of attaining to a state of felicitas in which God's presence is experienced for all eternity. However, there is also the concept of a transcendent moral goal which is experienced in this life, as it is expressed in the wisdom outlooks of Plato, Buddha, and Zarathusshtra.

For Plato, the goal of acting virtuously is to achieve a state of wisdom in which the philosopher directly contemplates the Good. For Buddha the goal was the state he called nirvana, while for Zarathushtra it was happiness and fulfilment in this life and immortality in the next. Underpinning all three perspectives is the view that acting morally leads to wisdom, and that experiencing wisdom is a transcendent state of being that is experienced here, in this world.

This leads to a fourth category of moral objectivism, which I'll call the mystical category.

THE MYSTICAL CATEGORY OF MORAL OBJECTIVISM

What is meant by the word "mystical"? Todaymystical tends to be used in a general sense in relation to unusual or mysterious perceptions experienced in a heightened emotional or sensory states. But mystical also has a more precise technical meaning.

The word mystical has its origin in the mysteries that were prevalent throughout the Mediterranean and Middle East in the centuries before and after the founding of Christianity. A central feature of the mysteries was an initiation through which the initiate came closer to the God or Goddess in whose name the mystery ceremony was conducted. The Greek name for such an initiate was *mustikos*. The idea was that an initiate had a higher form of experiential spiritual knowledge, and had literally entered the mystery within life. After the mysteries ceased to be practiced, the term mystic came to be used in relation to esoteric spiritual doctrines or highly specialized practices that developed within religions. These doctrines and practices include Talmud mysticism within the Judaic religion, Sufism within Islam, Vedanta within the Indian post-Vedic religions, and Christian mysticism. As the author of the classic work on mysticism, Evelyn Underhill, pointed out: "Mysticism, in its pure form, is the science of ultimates, the science of union with the Absolute, and nothing else, and the mystic is the person who attains to this union."[17]

Of course, not everyone believes in or accepts that mystical experiences exist or are real. Indeed, the great majority of academic philosophers and scientists reject the mystical perspective on empirical grounds, considering that the claims mystics make derive from experiences that are invalid because they cannot be experimentally verified by the senses. Equally problematic to rationalists is that mystics' claims to knowledge involve a hypothesis that there exists a God or a divine reality that can be experienced, yet even mystics acknowledge that that reality or God can not be logically proven. Twentieth century British philosopher, A.J. Ayer, represented this view when he observed:

> The fact that people have religious experiences is interesting from the psychological point of view, but it does not in any way imply that there is such a thing as religious knowledge. ... The theist, like the moralist, may believe that his experiences are cognitive experiences, but, unless he can formulate his 'knowledge' in propositions that are empirically verifiable, we may be sure that he is deceiving himself.[18]

Among researchers today there is an increasing openness towards what constitutes the verification of mystical states. This openness results in a large part from empirical research, which has measured the effect of mystical states on the brain in laboratory conditions.[19]

The processes which lead to mystical experiences, and the content of those experiences, have also been extensively documented by mystics themselves. Western culture possesses an extensive library of Judaic, Christian, and Islamic mystical literature from which derives a tradition of thought that is variously called the wisdom tradition, esoteric knowledge, or, as William James, the late-Victorian philosopher and psychologist, termed it, the perennial philosophy.

Underhill observed that mysticism has as its goal an experience of the transcendent spiritual reality. Mystics from different backgrounds have used very different terms in reference to this reality. For example, the Buddha used the term nirvana to refer to the transcendent reality that is experienced via mystical experience. He spoke little of the experience of nirvana in itself, on the grounds that its existence could only be confirmed through direct experience, not through logical argument. However, in one reference to it, he is reported to have stated:

> There is, monks, an unborn, an unbecome, an unmade, uncompounded. If, monks, there were not there this unborn, unbecome, unmade, uncompounded, there would not be here an escape from the born, the become, the made, the compounded.[20]

Zarathushtra called the transcendent reality Ahura Mazda. Unlike the Buddha's purely impersonal terminology, his concept of Ahura Mazda was both personal and impersonal: he addressed Ahura Mazda as "you" and referred to Ahura Mazda as "he," yet when describing Ahura Mazda's qualities he also used impersonal terms such as good thought, life, spirit, power, immortality, and wisdom. Nonetheless, in agreement with the Buddha, Zarathushtra was clear that Ahura Mazda was perceived inwardly:

> I have seen Ahura Mazda with my inner sight. ... This do I ask you, O Ahura, and wish you to tell me truly. How shall I attain my ecstatic goal, guided by you, which is reaching Mazda [wisdom] and becoming one with him? ... The person who desires inner light and tries to achieve it, O Mazda, do bestow it on him, through your holy and bright wisdom.[21]

Plato, too, held a mystic view that true knowledge transcended the sensual world, being apprehended inwardly by the philosopher. In his earlier dialogues he sometimes referred to a transcendent reality in personal, anthropomorphic terms. At other times he described it as good, beautiful, and true. In his late dialogues Plato called it the One and the Good. In his *Symposium*, Plato had Socrates describe the power of love to lift the philosophic lover above a sensual apprehension of physical beauty into a clearly mystical experience.

This beauty is first of all eternal; it neither comes into being nor passes away, neither waxes nor wanes ... nor again will this beauty appear to him like the beauty of a face or hands or anything else corporeal, or like the beauty of a thought or a science, or like beauty which has its seat in something other than itself, be it a living thing or the earth or the sky or anything else whatever; he will see it as absolute, existing alone within itself, unique, eternal ... Do you not see that in that region alone where he sees beauty with the faculty capable of seeing it, will he be able to bring forth not mere reflected images of goodness but true goodness, because he will be in contact not with a reflection but with the truth? And having brought forth and nurtured true goodness he will have the privilege of being beloved of God, and becoming, if ever a man can, immortal himself.[22]

From these quotations we can discern a number of features of mystic experiences. They involve a direct experience that transcends both rational thought and sense-based perception; while transcendent it is experienced inwardly; the experience may be described in language that utilizes either personal or impersonal terms, or both; the knowledge that derives from the mystic experience suggests that revelatory knowledge is not limited to the past, but may also be

---

THREE APPROACHES TO MYSTICAL MORAL OBJECTIVISM

ZARATHUSHTRA	BUDDHA	PLATO
• Goal: Ahura Mazda	• Goal: Nirvana	• Goal: The Good
• Transcends thought and sense perception	• Transcends thought and sense perception	• Transcends thought and sense perception
• Personal/impersonal	• Experiential	• Personal/impersonal
• Ahura Mazda achieved via inward experience	• Nirvana achieved via inward experience	• The Good achieved via inward experience
• Practice: Good thoughts, words, and deeds following the path of asha	• Practice: The Eightfold Nobel Path, ie. right thought, intention, etc	• Practice: Philosophic thought and living according to moral goods
• The highest moral good is wisdom	• The highest moral good is wisdom	• The highest moral good is wisdom

FIGURE 4.2

experienced today, in our here and now; and the means by which the mystic seeks to inwardly experience the transcendental includes love, humility, piety, worship, service, and a desire to be swept up into the divine.

Of course, this all sounds suitably high-minded. But what relevance does the mystical outlook have to how we live today?

CONCLUSIONS

Having introduced a range of perspectives on ethics and morality, we now need to pick our way through them and decide which is useful to us in our search for a moral yardstick that works for us today.

Our social reality is that we live in secular democracies founded on the principles of freedom and liberty. Our social ideals include freedoms of speech, thought, and movement, promote cultural pluralism, and function economically according to the principles of the free market. So no matter what our personal political, economic, ecological, religious, social, or sexual likes, dislikes or preferences, it is a given that very different viewpoints may exist together. Accordingly, as citizens we each have to exercise acceptance and tolerance of others just to get along.

On the other hand, what if we want to find out what really is right and wrong in our own and others' behavior? As independently existing moral beings we have no obligation to go along with what our society considers to be right and wrong—indeed, throughout history individuals have stood up and argued against widely and socially accepted behavior such as slavery and oppression that they decided was wrong. Each of us, as a citizen of a particular society, has the right to decide on moral issues for ourselves. Of this Peter Singer observes:

> Anyone who has thought through a difficult ethical decision knows that being told what our society thinks we ought to do does not settle the quandary. We have to reach our own decision. The beliefs and customs we were brought up with may exercise great influence on us, but once we start to reflect upon them we can decide whether to act in accordance with them, or to go against them.[23]

Further, it is clear that while money, the law, freedom of speech, and personal and political freedoms possess an element of the good, yet in themselves they can't provide us with goodness, fulfilment, happiness, or wisdom in our lives.

These are qualities that can't be legislated for, guaranteed by legal judgment, or put on the credit card. We have to find goodness, fulfilment, happiness, and wisdom for ourselves. Therefore, in practical terms, what we each require is a personal moral yardstick which we can use to guide our moral decision-making process while continuing to live in a morally relativist society.

I will now consider the ideas that were brought up in this and the previous two chapters with the purpose of picking though them to see what might be useful for establishing a moral yardstick that is relevant and useful to us today. Procedurally, Part 3 wil focus on the implications of moral relativism, while Part 4 will examine the implications of moral objectivism.

PART 3

HOW DOES THE GOOD WORK IN OUR LIVES?

CHAPTER 5

I'm Sorry, I Didn't Mean To Upset You

We saw in Part Two that, in part, contemporary Western moral relativism developed out of anthropologists' studies of non-Western cultures. They observed that other cultures had very different customs to those practiced in the West, involving class structures, the relative status of men and women, what constituted a crime, the administration of justice, the social rituals that accompanied entrance into adulthood, religious beliefs and practices, and attitudes towards sex and marriage.

Twentieth century anthropologists rejected the judgmental attitude towards these customs that had prevailed during the preceding colonizing period. Adopting the view that all customs are equally valid in their social contexts, they concluded that any particular culture's social norms, religious rituals, and customary social practices are neither good nor bad. Rather, they are just different, and are totally acceptable and right in the social context within which they are performed.

This kind of moral relativism currently prevails in the West. It has given rise to an attitude that considers right and wrong do not exist "out there" as absolutes, but are rather social constructs which are completely valid within the cultural contexts in which they are applied. Each culture decides what is right and wrong, lives according to the ethical strictures they have developed, and those in other cultures have no valid moral grounds to argue they are wrong.

On the surface this is a fine concept, because if we all lived according to the implications of moral relativism our lives would be harmonious. Of course, we don't. Instead, there is a great deal of inter-cultural friction within countries and between cultural groups.

This friction can be put under five headings: misunderstanding, self-defensiveness, being judgmental, social divergence, and individual divergence.

Two other social policies that have arisen from moral relativism are also con-
tentious, these being political correctness and affirmative action. I'll briefly examine these seven, because they reveal the principle difficulties relativist moral
perspectives face when they are applied in our everyday lives.

SEVEN DIFFICULTIES WITH MORAL RELATIVISM

Misunderstanding. This occurs when people don't understand the cultural perspective that gives rise to others' customary practices—such as Muslim women
wearing veils, or "foreigners" only eating foods prepared according to traditionally prescribed methods. At the darker end of the behavioral spectrum, misunderstanding gives way to suspicion, then to animosity. All these responses are
fuelled by ignorance of others' cultures and perspectives.

Self-defensiveness. This arises when people are insecure in themselves and
their beliefs, and have to attack others in order to boost their self-esteem. Insecurity can come from a number of psychological states and traits: from
ignorance, from fear (of the unknown culture, or of their own culture being
down-graded), from a lack of self-confidence, from a desire to protect vested
cultural interests (for example, when people don't want to admit the validity
of another's religious perspective because they want the superiority of their
own to remain undisputed), or from a desire to retain power.

Being judgmental. We all have an automatic tendency to evaluate others'
appearance, speech, or behavior. Some studies suggest we decide whether or
not we like people we have just been introduced to within seconds of meeting
them. Evolutionary theorists suggest this tendency may have developed
when our ancestors lived in small tribes and had to instantly decide whether
others they met were friendly or not. Today instant evaluation of others tends
to be according to the superficial criteria of bodily characteristics such as
looks, skin color, grooming, clothing, and accent. Slightly less crude criteria
of evaluation include income, occupation, social status, and the educational
facility in which we were schooled. This tendency may appear harmless, but
it becomes a moral liability when it is reinforced by ignorance, insecurity, fear,
misunderstanding and self-defensiveness, which cause evaluation to descend
into judgment and condemnation.

Social divergence. This occurs when one culture engages in customary
practices that those in another culture think are wrong. Examples include slav-

ery, blood revenge, and genital mutilation. Clearly, what those in one culture perceive as traditional behavior that is integral to their social functioning, those in another perceive as hurtful and, in agreement with Mill's "harm principle", wrong.

This disagreement is fraught with ethical complexities. For example, while it is easy to label an action wrong, in practice how "wrong" do we really believe it to be? We might argue murder is wrong, and that no customary practice that encourages murder can be acceptable. But in many countries blood revenge for perceived wrongs is a socially accepted practice: if a man's honour is impinged, he kills those responsible, including members of his own family (it is men who traditionally do the killing.)

Western citizens may consider justice systems that allow blood revenge to be morally repugnant. But some Western nations fund standing armies, and manufacture huge amounts of weaponry and munitions, which they not only use on peoples of other nations, but also sell knowing those who buy them intend to harm others. So who is the unethical party: those who use the munitions to harm, or those who manufacture and sell them in the first place? What moral high-ground can be adopted by those who manufacture munitions?

On the other hand, many nations are not convinced that blood-letting is the best way to address any situation morally. So socially divergent perceptions exist not only between Western and non-Western world, but also between Western citizens living in single nations.

Individual divergence. Citizens may diverge from their government regarding what the most effective ethical response in any situation should be. For example, a government may have a foreign policy based on military might, or on sanctions or negotiation, but individual citizens have the freedom to disagree with those policies. Similarly, citizens may disagree with the state's taxation policies, favoring either high taxation so the state has money to put towards social services, or low taxation, leaving poorer citizens to "sink or swim." If citizens strongly disagree with their country's social norms they can register their divergence via the media, the ballot box, the law court, or international organizations.

There are also two widely practiced implications of moral relativism: political correctness and affirmative action.

Political correctness. This is an attitude, enshrined in law in many countries, that has risen out of people's awareness of how derogatory, racist, or sexist language and behavior prevents some citizens from accessing the full range of freedoms a liberal democratic society should offer them.

Affirmative action. Affirmative action seeks to rebalance historical or social injustices, along with racial, gender, and ethnic discrimination, especially in the areas of education and employment. Corrective policies include the use of quotas, scholarships, and social programmes.

Both political correctness and affirmative action have been widely criticized on political, social, philosophic, religious, and economic grounds. But the reason they exist at all is because we realize that not all people within our society are treated as equals, and that social and economic freedoms, equality, and justice are not available to all on the same basis. Discrimination exists. Due to social, regional, racial, or cultural differences, the reality is that not all citizens have the same opportunities. Thus those in many countries have realized they could be doing much better for significant numbers of their socially and economically disadvantaged fellow citizens. Political correctness and affirmative action are two strategies for trying to achieve this.

Having defined these seven difficulties, I'll evaluate them.

CRITERIA ETHICAL BEHAVIOR NEEDS TO SATISFY

In order for moral relativism to function in a liberal, pluralistic, democratic culture, I suggest four criteria have to be satisfied.

First, it is undeniably the case that many customary practices are neither better nor worse than those practiced by other cultures; they are merely different. Thus they need at least to be tolerated by others.

Second, in deciding which customary practices to place in this first category, we can make use of Mills' harm principle, accepting and tolerating practices on the basis that they don't harm others. Hence because sex slavery and genital mutilation are harmful to those who are forced into them, they should not be accepted or tolerated. By the same reasoning, if the use of munitions such as landmines (which has become a customary practice in modern warfare), unexploded cluster bombs, and depleted uranium, causes far greater harm that what is justified by the immediate circumstances of warfare, then they should also be rejected as ethically unacceptable.

Third, while we live in morally relativist societies, many people still feel that some actions are definitely right and others definitely wrong. There are two senses in which this claim may be understood, one expansive, the other self-involved. Those adopting the view that certain behavior is right or wrong in the expansive sense do so by balancing their freedom of thought, speech, and action with a sense of responsibility to others in their society. Alternatively, those who view right and wrong in a self-involved sense wish to force their ethical views on everyone else. Those who practice the expansive sense are seeking a way to balance personal freedom and collective social responsibility; those who practice in the self-involved sense feel responsible only to their own (or perhaps their immediate community's) view of ethical behavior.

Fourth, for moral relativism to work in pluralist liberal democracies, each citizen has an obligation to make ethical distinctions between right and wrong

---

APPLYING MORAL RELATIVISM IN LIBERAL SECULAR DEMOCRACIES TODAY

SEVEN DIFFICULTIES WITH MORAL RELATIVISM	FOUR CRITERIA MORAL RELATIVISM NEEDS TO SATISFY
• We don't understand each other	• Citizens need to appreciate that many different social and cultural practices are not immoral, but merely different
• We unthinkingly defend our social norms because we are insecure	
• Defensiveness leads us to be judgmental, condemning others in order to justify our own views	• Citizens should reject social and cultural practices that harm others and consider them to be immoral
• We don't appreciate that the social practices of different culture naturally diverge from each other	• In deciding what is moral and immoral citizens need to adopt an expansive ethical view which includes respect for others and a sense of responsibility to others
• We diverge, as individuals, from what others in our own communities consider to be norms	
• Attempts to rebalance sexist, racist or prejudicial behavior descends into political correctness	• Citizens need to set aside their personal opinions and adopt an expansive ethical view, exchanging intolerance for tolerance, judgment for acceptance, etc
• Affirmative action is viewed as reverse discrimination	

FIGURE 5.1

in an expansive rather than a self-involved sense. This requires citizens to set aside their own views and to develop ethically from a self-involved to an expansive perspective. Such a change in perspective also requires developing from intolerant to tolerant, from being ignorant of others' perspectives to understanding what they are arguing for, and from automatically judging others to accepting difference. Citizens also need to drop fearful and insecure attitudes, and to instead develop rational thought, self-confidence, and self-esteem.

Ethical development thus has a psychological aspect, insofar as it requires people to grow out of limited, self-involved emotions such as fear, self-justification, and defensiveness, and to universalize their perspective. Without personal growth, citizens cannot fully participate in pluralist, liberal democracies.

This movement from self-involved to expansive involves a process of personal ethical development. Having concluded that for moral relativism to function in today's pluralist, liberal democracies, individual citizens need to develop from a self-involved to a universalizing ethical perspective, we now need to consider what a model for ethical development might look like. Developmental psychologist, Lawrence Kohlberg, has proposed such a model.[1]

A DEVELOPMENTAL APPROACH TO ETHICS

Kohlberg's model defines six stages of what he calls moral reasoning. These six stages indicate how an individual may develop the ability to function ethically in the contemporary Western social context.

The first two stages function on the level of what Kohlberg terms the pre-conventional. This is the egocentric "me first" attitude practiced by children and infantile adults. At the first stage such people only obey ethical rules out of fear, because they don't want to be caught and punished. Thus they do not recognize ethical standards, or possess any internal concept of good and bad. Kohlberg's second stage consists of self-interest, in which an individual is only interested in the behavior of others as far as it impacts on him or her.

Stages three and four function at the level of what Kohlberg terms the conventional, which is the level at which most adolescents and adults operate. On this level individuals assess right and wrong by comparing actions to social expectations. At the third stage people are aware of social roles, rules and relationships, and do their best to fulfil them, so they will be thought of as a "good boy" or "good girl". At the fourth stage people determine whether an action is moral or immoral by measuring it against their society's laws, dictums, and conventions. At stage three people are largely focussed on themselves, while at the fourth stage they start using rational thought to consider whether an action is right or wrong.

Stages five and six function on the post-conventional level. At stage five individuals function as independent moral entities, relying on their own judgment to assess the ethical implications of a situation. Mutual respect, impartiality, an ability to compromise, and an acceptance of the views of others are required for an individual to function at this stage. It can be seen that this is the stage at which an ethically responsible person needs to function in a liberal democracy. At the sixth stage the individual uses abstract reasoning to arrive at ethical assessments, much as Kant used his categorical imperative. Kohlberg had difficulty finding individuals who he considered functioned consistently at this level, suggesting that few people actually reach this final stage.

Kohlberg's model has been interrogated, endorsed, and doubted by numerous ethical thinkers. A significant question is whether his six stages can be

KOHLBERG'S SIX STAGES OF MORAL DEVELOPMENT

PRE-CONVENTIONAL
1. Egocentric. Obey rules out of fear of being punished.
2. Self-interested. Obey rules because there is something in it for them.

CONVENTIONAL
3. Goody two-shoes. Fulfil social norms of what constitutes good in order to be thought of as good.
4. Reasonably ethical. Considers behavior rationally by measuring it against rules, laws and conventions.

POST-CONVENTIONAL
5. Independent moral entity. Use their own judgment but balance self-interest by being impartial and respectful of others.
6. Abstract reasoner. Uses abstract thinking to make ethical decisions.

FIGURE 5.2

statistically verified, and whether they actually exist in reality. In formulating his six stages, Kohlberg was inspired by the work of Jean Piaget, whose educational studies and theories included considerations of children's ethical development. Kohlberg extended Piaget's thought, creating a model that remains significant because there are few other such models of ethical development.

One researcher who has offered an alternative model is Kohlberg's colleague, Carol Gilligan. Concerned that Kohlberg's model was centred on a justice-punishment view of morality, which she also saw as male-oriented, Gilligan suggested an "ethics of care" based on personal relationships rather than on concepts of justice. Accordingly, Gilligan has suggested a developmental model in which the first level of the pre-conventional is focussed on individual survival, the second level of the conventional involves self-sacrifice, and the third level of the post-conventional centres on non-violence. As integral philosopher Ken Wilber has observed with respect to Gilligan's perspective: "Gilligan found that men and women both move through three broad hierarchical stages of moral development, but that men tend to progress through these stages based more on judgments of rights and justice, whereas women tend to negotiate these hierarchical stages based on judgments of care and responsibility."[2]

Wilber himself calls these three levels the egocentric, sociocentric, and worldcentric. This is on the basis that individuals, whether they develop within the female-centred circle of care, or in the male-centred circle of justice, progressively expand their perspectives from the self, to the society, to the wider world.

Despite these variations in approaches, and despite Kohlberg's model not being experimentally verified, the point to take from either his model, or from Gilligan's alternative perspective, is the idea that there exists a developmental path by which people expand their ethical perspective from being wholly self-involved, through being idealistic, to developing a universalized point of view.

Hence we can see that in order for moral relativism to work in a practical sense it requires both a culture as a whole, and individuals within that culture, to grow from an ethically self-involved moral infant to an ethically socially responsible, independently thinking and functioning moral adult.

CHAPTER 6

Are Customary Practices Moral?

We have observed that human responses to ethical situations start at egocentric, extend through sociocentric, and are fulfilled at world-centric (to use Wilber's terms). This suggests there exists a developmental scale for ethical decision-making. But what about customary practices? Where do they fit in?

Customary practices include cultural observances, such as national holidays that celebrate or mourn significant national events, religious rituals, rules regarding social etiquette, sexual activity, and marriage. We tend to automatically accept that it is good for us individually and as a society to observe such practices, to the extant that social pressure is placed on individuals to conform and to observe them with everyone else. Those who do not observe such customs are viewed as non-conformists, at best, or ostracized or punished, at worst.

But how moral are customary practices really? Are all customary practices morally equal? Or do they, as with ethical decision-making, fit into a graduated scale? Should customary practices be situated into the low or high end of ethical behavior? Or are some practices at one end, and others at the other?

To begin with, even a cursory glance indicates that all customary practices can't be considered to be equal. Blood revenge and genital mutilation are not of the same order as wearing traditionally-prescribed clothing, eating religiously approved foods, or engaging in communal rituals. From this we would expect customary practices to extend along a graduated ethical scale.

In addition, some customary practices are performed on purely traditional grounds, having been observed for thousands of years. For example, Zoroastrians in India (where they are called Parsis) place the newly dead on high wooden platforms for vultures to pick the flesh from the bones. This funerary practice dates back to at least 6,000 BCE, with depictions of the same practice being preserved on walls of ancient buildings in the excavated Turkish city of Catal Hüyük.[4] The funerary practice of burying the deceased body rather than cremating it goes back even further.

Our hunter-gatherer forebears believed that the animals they killed would be reborn from their bones. Accordingly, Chugach Eskimos leave the skull of a bear they have killed in the place it died, because they believe the animal's soul is in the skull and that the dead bear will be reborn from it. This same belief has been traced back to 75,000 BCE, due to evidence that the ancient hunters of cave bears ritually preserved the skulls of the bears they killed for the same reason.[5] It can be seen, then, that the Christian and Islamic idea that at the end of time dead believers will be resurrected from their bones, and therefore that bodies should be buried and not cremated, is extremely old.

Other customary practices are centred on taboos. Many taboos are to do with food, with numerous religions prescribing what worshippers may or may not eat, and when. For example, Judaism and Islam forbid the eating of pork on the grounds they are unclean, while Hindus have a prohibition against eating any meat—although the Brahmin priests once ate the flesh of the cows as part of their religious ceremonies. Early Christianity declared Friday a day of abstinence in recognition of the fact that Christ was crucified on a Friday. On Christian abstinence days the flesh of bird and beast was not allowed to be consumed, nor was butter, milk, cheese and other animal derivatives. Therefore fish became a traditional Friday meal. Muslims practice Ramadan, a fast Islam adopted from Judaism, in which no food or drink is consumed during daylight hours over the period of a month. Lent, the Christian equivalent, prescribes what believers may or may not eat during the forty days leading up to Easter. At other times customary practices involve feasting rather than taboos, such as Eid at the end of Ramadan, the Christian Feast of the Ascension that celebrates the end of Lent, and agricultural feasts that accompanied the harvest in ancient times.

Other customary practices focus on cleanliness. Among Maori, tabletops are considered to be *tapu* (sacred) and are not to be sat on. Besides the symbolic religious significance of this injunction, it expresses a practical concern for keeping food away from uncleanness. Similarly, in Islam worshippers have to wash their face and hands before praying. As Muslims pray five times a day, quite apart from the religious symbolism involved in the action of washing, that religious injunction had the practical effect of institutionalizing cleanliness—at a time when those in Europe scarcely bathed from one year to the next. Many religions quarantine women during their periods, on the grounds of a taboo against what is considered to be polluted blood.

However, other customary practices just appear to be arbitrary, as for example the wearing or not wearing of hats during religious ceremonies. In Judaism and Islam worshippers are required to cover their heads, while different Christian sects advocate a variety of practices, with the clergy and male female worshippers variously wearing or not wearing head-coverings over the centuries. In the seventeenth century Englishman George Fox, who founded the Quakers, was beaten and imprisoned for not doffing his hat to his social superiors. Fox considered all men and women to be equals, whatever their sex or class, and argued that there was no moral requirement to conform to his era's customary practices of doffing hats. For this "unethical" behavior, Fox and many of his followers were sent to prison. Fox's response was to petition the English Parliament for decades to promote social tolerance. His approaches eventually succeeded. In 1689 the British Parliament ratified the Act of Toleration which allowed freedom of religious expression to dissenters from the Church of England (with the exception of Catholics). Suddenly, behavior that had been unethical for decades was no longer so.

This leads to the question of whether customary practices have any moral value, or are just arbitrary social behavior in which some societies engage and others don't. Obviously, there are many reasons why customary practices come to be widely accepted, and why performing them establishes people as ethically good. But beyond social approval, is there really any real moral weight behind them? This question becomes even more relevant when we realize that customary practices change over time, may come to be viewed by later generations as irrelevant (as happened with the wearing of hats) or even wrong (i.e. slavery), and accordingly become optional or are discarded as unethical.

CUSTOMARY PRACTICES AS SOCIAL CONSTRUCTS

The Fourth Way teacher, G.I. Gurdjieff, considered that customary practices, and the ethical standards associated with them, constituted "subjective morality." By this term he meant that the concepts of what constitute good or bad change according to social circumstances, religious beliefs, how people view the world, and what new social ideas have been adopted. Consequently good and bad are themselves arbitrary concepts. As Gurdjieff's pupil, P.D. Ouspensky, put it:

> What is morality? Understanding the laws of conduct? It is not sufficient. … What is good? What is bad? Generally, … man borrows moral principles from religious, philosophical or scientific ideas, or simply adopts conventional taboos. He believes that some things are good and some things are bad. But this is subjective morality, and the understanding of good and evil is purely relative. In all countries and all epochs certain moral codes were accepted which tried to explain what is good and what is bad. But if we try to compare the existing theories we shall see that they all contradict one another and are full of contradictions in themselves. … So, if you think about this problem, you will understand that in spite of hundreds of moral systems and teachings man cannot say what is right and what is wrong, for moral values change, there is nothing permanent in them.[5]

This is a commonsense way of looking at customary practices. When we live entirely inside a culture we tend to unthinkingly accept the norms regarding what constitutes good and bad behavior that our culture advocates. But when we view concepts of good and bad from outside our culture, and especially if we become emotionally alienated from aspects of our culture, then we start to see how much of a social construct they are. We may accept customary practices because we enjoy them, or see no harm in them. Conversely, we may see them as deficient and reject them. But, in the end, what weight should we give to customary practices in the context of the moral yardstick we are seeking here?

Ethical concepts that derive from customary practices are clearly conventional—in Kohlberg's sense of conventional morality being based on fulfilling social roles and conforming to society's rules and laws. Of course, what is conventional in one era is not so in another. Thus in the past being conventional meant doing what parents, elders, and social role models did. These days being conventional is often the opposite of this, with conventional teenage behavior rejecting the ethical standards advocated by parents and elders, and instead doing what their peers, "cool" role models, and famous people do. Either way, it is all conventional behavior.

However, while acting conventionally has its pleasures—whether it involves wearing certain items of clothing in a certain way, eating certain foods in a long-accustomed manner, or gathering in communal and peer groups and together engaging in common social, religious, or communal rituals —none of this has anything to do with moral values. As long as we obey the law and do not harm others, we may choose to do as others do out of respect or enthusiasm for their traditions, or we may choose not to do so—but none of this has anything to do with ethical values. People may approve of or attack others who do or don't act as they choose to do, or speak as they speak, or think as they think—but, again, there is no moral basis for their approval or attack.

Similarly, people may justify their customary practices by claiming God commanded them to carry them out, and therefore that not to do so would be immoral. However, customary practices are invented by human beings. So just because they are practices religious worshippers agree are good to carry out doesn't mean they are not all further instances of arbitrary behavior.

Of course, none of this is bad. It doesn't mean we shouldn't respect others for doing what they do. Nor does it mean that we shouldn't join in with them. But neither are such practices ethically good or bad. Ultimately, they are ethically neutral, being no more than what people choose to do.

So from the perspective of this study, customary practices must be seen as socially agreed ideas and behavior that are based in moral relativism. Most customary practices, however widely adhered to, are founded on arbitrary concepts and behaviors. Many are ethically neutral. Others are fetters with which we bind others—and thus ourselves. All this means that customary practices must be rejected as a yardstick for deciding what is ultimately good and bad.

Accordingly, I arrive at the final question that must be asked of moral relativism. Given the arbitrariness that appears to be basic to all ethical perspectives derived from the various forms of moral relativism, is there any ethical value associated with moral relativism that could give us a reasonable foundation for assessing what is ethically acceptable and what is unacceptable? Can we draw from moral relativism any ethical concept that we could use in relation to the moral yardstick we seek? This is what I will consider next.

CHAPTER 7

Measuring Up To The Good

What has been concluded so far is that being a morally good citizen in pluralist liberal, secular democracies involves living with our fellow citizens in an harmonious manner, being tolerant, respecting and accepting others' beliefs and customary practices, and allowing others the freedom to think, say, and do as they wish—as long, of course, as they don't harm others, and their actions are lawful.

On the other hand, as free-thinking citizens, we are not obliged to automatically agree with what others think, say, or do. Clearly, a proportion of people in any complex society lie, cheat, exploit, and harm others. So it is naive to be completely accepting of all our fellow citizens' actions, whether they be business people, politicians, religious leaders, media figureheads, or our neighbors.

As Kant observed, we are each morally autonomous, free to make up our own mind respecting what is ethical or unethical. Indeed, it could be added that it is our obligation as citizens to think through the ethical choices that affect both us personally and our community as a whole.

The question then becomes, what criteria should we use to decide what is ethical or not? We have seen that the moral yardsticks past thinkers have come up include making ethical decisions by using the categorical imperative (Kant), on the basis of the greatest happiness principle (Bentham), by using the harm principle (Mill), by seeking individual happiness through rationalized self-interest (Rand), and by universalizing self-interested decision-making (Singer).

What unites all these thinkers, and underpins the forms of moral relativism that we have been examining, is the concept of secular humanism. That is, all these thinkers place human experience and rationality at the centre of their thinking about ethics. In doing so, they reject the idea that humanity should rely on any transcendent or supernatural source of ethical knowledge. They emphasize instead that we must each decide for ourselves how we should live with each other, and therefore what thoughts, words, and deeds are right and which are wrong.

The humanist outlook dates back in Western thought to the Greeks. Protagoras argued, "Man is the measure of all things". Similarly, while in Plato's writings Socrates emphasized the need for us to use rational thought to decide for ourselves what values we should live by. In the twelfth century, Aquinas and other Catholic Scholastic thinkers looked back to the Greeks. So while they considered that knowledge ultimately came by revelation from God, they adopted the Greek emphasis on rational thought, which they considered could validly be used to understand the ways of God in the world.

During the Renaissance, this appreciation developed further. A new movement emphasizing a humanist outlook emerged in Italy in the twelfth century. This new outlook diminished the significance of divine revelation, emphasising instead the role human thought can play in understanding the world. Over the following several hundred years, humanist thought became so integrated into European culture that education shifted from being theologically-centred on Christian thought, and instead developed a curriculum that we today call the liberal arts. The liberal arts included history, poetry, rhetoric, grammar, and moral philosophy, and their primary texts were non-Christian Greek and Roman writings. Underpinning this curriculum was a new emphasis on developing human potential. Where traditional Christianity assumed humanity's sinfulness and shame as a result of original sin, humanism assumed humanity's nobility. This positive humanist outlook is reflected in Hamlet's famous speech: "What a piece of work is man! How noble in reason! How infinite in faculties! In form and moving, how express and admirable! In action how like an angel! In apprehension, how like a god! The beauty of the world! The paragon of animals!"

During the Ages of Reason and Enlightenment this high regard for human capacity was taken even further. Rational thought, as it manifested in the scientific method, shifted the West's cultural focus from a supernatural God to an empirically experienced nature. Morally, Kant argued that human beings should take onto themselves responsibility for the ethical outcome of their actions. We human beings no longer needed God to tell us what to think and how to act; rational thought gave us the power to decide for ourselves. We no longer needed to report to God; we had our fellow human beings to whom we had now to be responsible. The Utilitarian outlook was a natural progression from this perspective, as was the secular, liberal societies that we live in today. Thus while the ethical outlook for Western societies is moral relativism, underlying this is humanism. So where does this take us with respect to finding an moral yardstick?

It means that in a society that is dominated by moral relativism we must look towards humanity itself as a measure for what is right or wrong. Therefore the criteria by which the ethical value of a decision may be assessed becomes: *Does this moral decision, and its resultant action, enhance our humanity, or does this decision diminish our humanity?* Because we are morally autonomous beings, living communally with others, we have a social responsibility to live harmoniously with them. Hence the consequences of our actions can be discerned as good when they enhance our shared humanity, and as bad when they diminish our shared humanity.

What is meant by "our shared humanity"? Drawing on the conclusions I drew in relation to Kohlberg's model, it may argued that "humanity" is a developmental concept, in the sense that just as we are physically not born adults but grow into adults, so we are not born with a sophisticated moral sensibility, we have to grow into it. Such growth involves, as both Kant and Singer have pointed out, moving beyond narrow self-interest, putting aside our own likes

---

CONCLUSIONS REGARDING MORAL RELATIVISM

- Ethical actions enhance our humanity. Unethical actions do not.
- Many social norms and traditional and customary practices are ethically neutral, neither enhancing nor diminishing our humanity. They are just things people do with each other.
- Ethics involves a developmental scale, with decision-making growing from self-interested and self-involved to embracing a universalizing process of rational decision-making.
- Ethical behavior requires each citizen, at a minimum, to be tolerant and accepting of others. Ideally, understanding should underpin responses.

FIGURE 7.1

and dislikes, and using rational thought to universalize our ethical decision-making process. Accordingly, narrow self-interest that disregards the impact of decision-making on others, and that especially has a dehumanizing impact, cannot be ethically good. It is only by using rational thought to universalize our decision-making process that can we can grow ethically from children to adults.

Thus, while social norms, agreed rules, and customary practices play a significant part in our interaction as human beings, in the terms we are discussing here they remain secondary factors with respect to deciding what is ethical. It isn't whether what we are doing conforms to social norms, rules, or customary practices that makes our actions good; it is whether our actions enhance our own and our fellow citizens' humanity. Customary practices that advocate genital mutilation or slavery can be categorized as ethically bad because they diminish the humanity of those who are mutilated—as well as of those who do the mutilating. On the other hand, if a social norm dictates that the wealthier should share their money with poorer citizens via taxes or charity, and if that money helps the poorer develop their human potential, then that action is ethically good.

PART 4

IS THERE A GOOD TO STEER OUR LIFE BY?

CHAPTER 8

How Bad Can We Really Be?

Moral objectivism provides us with objective criteria for deciding what is good or bad. The assumption behind them is that these criteria transcend our subjective, self-involved perspective. Historically religions have provided humanity with these objective criteria, which they derived from (or justified by using) supernatural revelation. But as we saw in Chapter Four, philosophic thinkers have also suggested non-religious objective criteria for assessing whether actions are ethical or not.

In this and the next two chapters, I will examine key issues involved in the claims made by thinkers who support both religious and non-religious objective moral perspectives. These are: the concept of original sin, moral codes, conscience, and the way that the idea of an afterlife has impacted on our thinking about the purpose of being moral. I'll start start with the concept of original sin.

ARE WE REALLY "BAD TO THE BONE"?

The global media makes us very aware that people are daily harming, exploiting, and killing others through oppression, by engaging in sectarian and ethnically-based violence, by supporting political and religious differences, and for money, possessions, and resources. If we believe in a knowing, loving, and good God, we wonder how it could be that so many apparently innocent men, women, and children are treated so badly. Then we start thinking that, since a good God couldn't be responsible for so much suffering and death, maybe there exists an anti-God force in the world that is really responsible for all the pain, suffering, and misery. We popularly call this force evil. But we human beings also create pain, misery, and suffering for others through our actions. Traditionally, such actions have been called sinful.

So we end up with two ideas: evil rampages through the world outside us, and sin rampages within us. Further, evil exists independently of God, and sin keeps us separate from God. We are all familiar with the concept of original sin, that Adam and Eve's eating an apple from the tree of knowledge of good and evil in the Garden of Eden has resulted in all humanity being born with evil in them and with a natural propensity towards sinning.

The idea that God is good, and therefore that if evil exists in the world then it can only exist separate from God—that is, God is one thing and evil something else—is an idea that was thought up at a relatively recent stage of our common cultural development. It is not an idea that was present in early religions. So where did this dualistic good-bad outlook come from? Who first thought it up?

The answer is that Zarathushtra did, by postulating the idea that dual and opposed forces animate the world. Zarathushtra conceived of one force as good, which he associated with Spenta Mainyu, the holy or beneficial spirit, and the other as bad, associated with Angra Mainyu, the evil or hurtful spirit. It must be noted that Zarathushtra did not identify Ahura Mazda, the eternal and transcendent God, with either the good or the bad. Nor did Angra Mainyu exist separate from, and in opposition to, Ahura Mazda. Rather, Zarathushtra called these two spirits twins. They both existed in Ahura Mazda and in the world Ahura Mazda had created.

Martin Haug, a German scholar who was among the first Westerners to study the Zoroastrian religion in depth, observed: "Having arrived at the grand idea of the unity and indivisibility of the Supreme Being, he [Zarathushtra] undertook to solve the great problem that has engaged the attention of so many wise men ... viz. how are the imperfections discoverable in the world ... compatible with the goodness, holiness, and justice of God? This great thinker of remote antiquity solved this difficult question by the supposition of two primeval causes, which though different, were united, and produced the world of material things, as well as that of spirit. ... The one who produced the 'reality' is called *vohu manah*, 'the good mind'; the other, through whom the 'non-reality' originated, bears the name *aka manah*, 'the evil mind'. ... They are the two moving causes in the universe united from the beginning, and therefore called 'twins.'"[1]

The moral implications for human beings, and the practical reason for Zarathushtra's conceptual demarcation between these opposed but intertwined twins, is that in life we are faced with a fundamental moral choice: we can choose to go the way of the good spirit, or we can choose to go the way of the bad spirit. Whichever we choose, our thoughts, words and deeds become filled with that chosen spirit. As Zarathushtra wrote:

> Reflect with clear purpose, each man for himself, on the two choices. ... Truly, there are two primal Spirits, twins long known to be in conflict. In thought, word, and act they are two: the good and the bad. Those who act well have chosen rightly between them; not so the evil-doers. When these two Spirits came together, they created Life and non-Life. At the end the Worst Existence shall be for the wicked, but (the House of) Best Purpose shall be for the just man. ... He who makes better or worse his thoughts, O Mazda, he by act and word (makes better or worse) his Inner Self; she [the Inner Self] follows his leanings, wishes and likings.[2]

There are some familiar ideas here. Zarathushtra considered we have free will to choose the path of good or the path of evil, and therefore to make our inner self morally better or morally worse. What we choose in this life then dictates where we go in the next, either to the House of Good Purpose, which is also called the House of Song, or to the House of Worst Existence. Two further ideas are significant to this discussion.

First, on the metaphysical level, the twins are conceived of as reality and non-reality, or life and non-life. As already pointed out, Angru Mainyu does not exist independently of the Good Spirit. Instead, it is conceived as the absence of good, and of the absence of reality or of life. The assumption Zarathushtra is making is that the world is fundamentally good, and human beings living in the world naturally participate in this good. It is only through choice that we move away from good, into unreality and non-life. There is clearly no place here for original sin. Quite the opposite. If we wish to think in such terms, we rather partake of "original good."

The second significant idea is on the psycho-spiritual level of mind and thought. Zarathushtra wrote: "He who makes his thoughts better or worse, O Mazda, he by act and word (makes better or worse) his Inner Self; she follows his leanings, wishes, and likings." That is, we create life and non-life, reality and unreality, through our own good or evil thoughts, and our thoughts in turn shape our inner self. Our inner self then manifests outwardly in our thoughts, words and deeds. Thus while Zarathushtra conceived of two metaphysical and moral tendencies existing in the world, we have responsibility for which we choose and therefore what we become. The content of our mind is key.

Interestingly, Zarathushtra's concept of the mind is very close to that of the Buddha, who considered that controlling the mind was a key to living the good life and achieving nirvana:

> When you wish to know that all things, inner and outer, are produced by your own mind … make a thorough survey of all the different aspects of the self-discriminating mind. … The Mind is the leader of all things, because all things of the world are created by the Mind. … When the Mind is disturbed, the multiplicity of things is produced; when the Mind is quieted the multiplicity of things disappears. … When the Mind runs wild it is like a violent elephant; one thought follows the other with the quickness of lightning; when the mind loses its composure it moans like an agile monkey and thus becomes the origin of all evils.[3]

For the Buddha, as for Zarathushtra, there was no original sin. Instead, he considered that we are the creators, in our inner self, of good and evil which result from our own choices.

Zoroastrian ideas influenced the development of Judaism through the time Jewish exiles spent in Babylon—Zoroastrianism was the Babylonian state religion. This influence is seen in the Judaic idea that there exist in us two tendencies, one towards good (*yetzer ha-tov*), the other towards evil (*yetzer hara*), but with both being manifestations of God's will. This same idea of a dualistic choice emanating from a single source is also present in Islam, in which humanity is offered the choice of accepting or rejecting the guidance of Allah, with the result that they divide into believers or unbelievers, the happy or unhappy, the knowledgeable or ignorant, the tormented or peaceful.

Two paths. Two ways of thinking. Two ways of speaking. Two ways of doing. Two ways of living. And we each have a choice as to which path we walk.

THE ORIGIN OF ORIGINAL SIN

What about original sin? Where did it come from? In adopting original sin as a moral concept, Christianity is the odd religion out among its companion Abrahamic religions. While both Judaism and Islam consider humanity has a tendency to stray morally, neither goes so far as to condemn humanity at birth. As a doctrine, original sin is a post-Christ addition to Christian theology. It is not present in the *Gospels*, Jesus Christ didn't teach it, and while Paul of Tarsus refers to human sin beginning in the Garden with Adam and Eve, he didn't draw from this a doctrine of original sin. Instead, Augustine and the Church Fathers invented the concept in the third and fourth centuries after Christ.

The Church Fathers used a Jewish story of origins to create the doctrine of original sin (even though Jewish religious teachers themselves had never drawn from it the conclusion that humanity was fundamentally bad). They decided they needed it because Jesus Christ was a savior god, so Christianity needed a theological explanation regarding what Christ was saving humanity from. Christ came and was crucified to repay humanity's spiritual debt of innate sinfulness that derived from Adam and Eve disobeying God in the Garden of Eden. So the concept of original sin (drawn from the Old Testament), and the salvation through Christ that balanced it (presented in the New Testament), gave Christianity a significant theological point of difference from other religions of the time that also offered worshippers a savior god.

In addition, Zarathushtra's dualistic outlook was undoubtedly a key influence on Augustine himself. Before his conversion to Christianity, Augustine followed Manichaeism, a religion that extended Zarathushtra's dualistic notions by teaching that there is a spiritual realm of light and a material realm of darkness. Manichaeism identified the human spirit with light and the good, and the human body with darkness and evil. According to Manichaeism salvation was achieved when practitioners rose above their material body and came to know their true, spiritual self. After he converted to Christianity, Augustine denounced Manichaeism vociferously. But it is clear that he drew on Zarathushtra's dualism, which he had processed via Manichaeism, for his concept of original sin.

Karen Armstrong, a historian of religions, has argued that the Manichean idea that the body was evil was psychologically internalized by Augustine. He considered that a human being's ability to think rationally was reduced by physical feelings and sensations, and especially by sexual sensations. He then identified the barbarian hordes from northern Europe who, during his lifetime, were attacking and destroying the Roman Empire, with bodily sensations. As Armstrong observes, "this image of reason dragged down by the chaos of sensations and lawless passions [as experienced in sex] was disturbingly similar to

Rome, source of rationality, law and order in the West, overrun by barbarian tribes."[4]

Under his rational surface Augustine was much like any thinking person today: a disturbed man living in disturbing times. However, whether the cause was the Manichean view of the body as spiritually tainted, or his personal discomfort with his own sexuality, it was his decision to accentuate the role of Eve in the downfall of "mankind," and to use this story to justify his view that all women were bad. Not that Augustine was alone in this view. Many of the Church Fathers shared Augustine's distrust of sex, and were equally revolted by women, leading them to collectively decide that women were temptresses, and that Eve was responsible for Adam's transgression in the Garden of Eden and therefore for humanity's fall.

So strong were these ideas in Augustine that he couldn't understand why God had created Eve in the first place: "If it was good company and conversation that Adam needed, it would have been much better to have two men together as friends, not a man and a woman."[5] So it was out this mixture of sexual unease, the Manichian condemnation of the body, and his fears for Rome's future, that Augustine concocted his dark view of humanity's moral nature:

> Banished (from Paradise) after his sin, Adam bound his offspring also with the penalty of death and damnation, that offspring which by sinning he had corrupted in himself, as in a root; so that whatever progeny was born (through carnal concupiscence, by which a fitting retribution for his disobedience was bestowed upon him) from himself and his spouse—who was the cause of his sin and the companion of his damnation—would drag through the ages the burden of Original Sin, by which it would itself be dragged through manifold errors and sorrows. ... So the matter stood; the damned lump of humanity was lying prostrate, no, was wallowing in evil, it was falling headlong from one wickedness to another; and joined to the faction of the angels who had sinned, it was paying the most righteous penalty of its impious treason.[6]

The idea that original sin has tainted humanity, making us all at the least naturally inclined to sin, and at the worst evil creatures damned forever, was undoubtedly a factor that led to Europe's Enlightenment thinkers rejecting Christianity. They and those who followed them had a brighter, more optimistic view of humanity, and held great hopes for what humanity might achieve. The doctrine of original sin contradicted this, forcing humanity to keep looking back into the past, and to hang its collective head in shame, instead of looking forwards, into the future, with shining, hope-filled eyes.

Given all this, does original sin have any place in our search for a moral yardstick by which to live our lives? Clearly, the concept of original sin has had an enormous impact of the Western psyche. Nonetheless, it is nothing more than an idea invented by a group of men at a certain time in history. And while it has remained an influential theological concept for almost two thousand years, and continues to appeal to people who wish to emphasize their own and everyone else's spiritual limitations, culturally, spiritually, and psychologically the West has moved on from this self-flagellating view of human existence.

Accordingly, we can conclude that the concept of original sin, being no more than a cultural construct, is of no use to us in our search for a moral yardstick by which to live in the modern world.

WHAT ABOUT THE WAY WE TREAT EACH OTHER?

However, this is not the end of this issue. Because while we may reject original sin as a moral concept, there is still the issue that behind it lies an undeniable truth of human existence: that there is much in our treatment of each other, of other living creatures, and of the planet, that is unthinking and destructive. In sombre moments, we may even consider that perhaps it is not just that human beings occasionally and unthinkingly lapse into acts of hurt and violence, but that there is something intrinsically wrong with humanity as a whole.

Thus Augustine's idea of original sin could be seen as a manifestation of a profound sense of unease that arises when we contemplate the human condition. We may disagree with the way he formulated it, but that doesn't mean Augustine's insight into humanity's unease isn't worth considering.

This unease is present in the way that, as Zarathushtra saw it, human beings so often choose to enter the House of Worst Existence and to embrace non-life and the unreal. Like many other religious prophets, Zarathushtra himself felt the impact of those who embraced non-life, being hounded by enemies. The Buddha considered that human beings were lost in *samsara* (the cycle of birth, decay, and death), and that our bodily desires, destructive emotions, and arbitrary thoughts keep us in ignorance, living in illusion. Plato elaborated a famous metaphor for the human condition in *The Republic*, in which he described human beings as sitting in a cave, with their backs to the entrance and to the light, so that all they perceive are shadows of things moving beyond the cave's entrance that reflected on the cave's rear wall. For Plato, human beings lived in delusion and shadows, their backs turned to reality. Each of Zarathsutra, Buddha, and Plato therefore possessed a clear vision of humanity living an uneasy existence in which we all too readily embrace the negative possibilities of life.

This same uneasiness with human existence is also present in other, non-religious lines of thought. For example Robert Ardrey, in his once-applauded 1960s book, *African Genesis,* argued that humanity evolved out of killer apes. He considered the killer genes that we inherited from those apes live on inside us today, causing us to be the aggressive, destructive species that we are (our killer ape ancestry is depicted in the opening scenes of Arthur C. Clark and Stanley Kubrick's film *2001, A Space Odyssey*). This theory has been debunked by anthropologists and geneticists. Nonetheless, it excited interest at the time because it reflected the unease many felt at the way the Cold War threatened to extinguish human existence altogether, and offered an explanation for such irrational behavior. This theory continues today in another form, in which scholars argue that the Neanderthals died off so suddenly because they were exterminated by our killer Cro-Magnon ancestors.

ANCIENT WARRIOR CULTURES

Another influential idea, derived from archaeological research, is that there was a turning point in human prehistory, from around 3500 BCE, when the peaceful Neolithic farmers of Europe and the Middle East were invaded by a proto-Indo-European warrior culture. Archeologist Marija Gimbutas, who was the first to offer this theory, argued that this invasion completely changed European and Middle Eastern cultures, transforming their social structure, outlook, and religions from peaceful and Goddess-centred into warring, class divided, and God-centred. Gimbutas suggested that this invading proto-Indo-European culture originated from the steppes region around the southern shores of the Black Sea, and spread east and south in three waves into Iran and South-Eastern Europe from 3,400 BCE to 2,100 BCE.

The proto-Indo-Europeans were characterized by a tripartite social structure of priests, warriors, and peasants. A tribal, pastoral people, they were ruled by a king who was often also the head priest, and worshipped male thunder gods (which manifested in later cultures as Zeus, Thor, Indra, and Jupiter). The gods referred to in the Indian religious texts, the *Vedas*, and the clan wars recounted in the *Mahabharata*, reflect this warrior and thunder god culture, as do the warrings recounted in the ancient Jewish historical books, Homer's *Iliad*, and the mythologies and histories of all Eastern, Middle-eastern and European cultures of the past several thousand years. The significance of Gimbutas' argument for this study is that she considered that the proto-Indo-Europeans changed humanity's lifestyle from peaceful, matrilinear, cooperative, and agricultural, into aggressive, class-structured, and war-making:

> The Old European and Indo-European belief systems are diametrically opposed. The Indo-European society was war-like, exogamic, patriarchal, pratilinear, and patrilocal, with a strong clanic organization and social hierarchy which gave prominence to the warrior class. Their main gods were male and depicted as warriors. There is no possibility that this pattern of social organization could have developed out of the Old European matrilinear, matricentric, and endogamic balanced society. Therefore, the appearance of the Indo-Europeans in Europe represent a collision of two ideologies.[7]

In the 1970s Raine Eisler took these ideas even further, proposing that the war-like culture we have today derives from the warrior Indo-Europeans who took over the previously peaceful, co-operative Goddess culture and turned co-operation into competition, and peaceful egalitarian interactions into male-focused competitive struggles for social status and power.[ao] She called these warrior cultures "dominator societies."

There is considerable doubt among scholars as to the validity of Gimbutas and Eisler's ideas. For example, the city of Jericho, which dates back to 9,000 BCE, was surrounded by walls, apparently built to keep troublesome people out, which argues against an entirely peaceful agrarian culture at this time. In acknowledgement of this, Eisler has since softened her views, agreeing that the historical archaeological record shows violence dating back before 3,500 BCE. Nonetheless, it is the case that there is extensive evidence for warring throughout the Middle East from the late Bronze Age, when warriors commanded by kings undoubtedly invaded and massacred foreign populations and committed bloody punishment on their own unruly fellow citizens.

And, inarguably, mythological recounting of this degeneration from gentile agriculturalist to killer warrior is present in the many tales of violence among the gods (Zeus become leader of the Greek gods by castrating and murdering his father). It is also present in the Greek myth that humanity once lived in a golden age, then fell progressively through ages of silver and bronze, until we are now in the lowest age, that of iron. Vedic literature describes this same fall through a series of four yuga, with the present era being kali yuga. Both myths asert that humanity once lived a peaceful, fruitful, pure, happy, and immortal existence. In comparison, today's age is one of darkness, ignorance, discord, warring, and death.

THE MYTH OF REDEMPTIVE VIOLENCE

Christian theologian, Walter Wink, takes Eisler's idea of dominator societies one step further again by arguing that we in the West live in a Dominator System, which "is characterized by unjust economic relations, oppressive political relations, biased race relations, patriarchal gender relations, hierarchical power relations, and the use of violence to maintain them all."[9] Wink considers that violence has become so profoundly ingrained in the fabric of how we live that not only do we accept unbalanced and oppressive power relations in our lives, but we also unthinkingly agree to war as the right and correct way to "resolve conflict":

> After 3,000 BCE we encounter evidence of warfare on a grand scale. Social systems became rigidly hierarchical, authoritarian, and patriarchal. ... In culture after culture, human destiny was driven in a direction few would have consciously chosen. Plunder from conquests gave rise to new classes of aristocrats and priests who produced nothing. Their survival in turn depended on ever new conquests. Societies found themselves locked in a struggle for dominance from which no one could escape. Defence against a powerful aggressor required a society to become more like the society that threatened it. If the attackers wielded swords and their victims had only hoes, it became a matter of urgency that the victims arm themselves with the newer weapons. ... No one person or group of people imposed the Dominator System on us; it came wholly uninvited. People simply stumbled into a struggle for power beyond their ability to avoid it or to stop it.[10]

Underpinning the Dominator System is what Wink calls "the myth of redemptive violence." Wink dates this myth back to the violent and murderous overthrow of the ancient regime of Mesopotamian gods by a younger generation led by Marduk. Wink considers this myth presents a narrative in which a hero is beaten by the bad guy, almost to death, but then makes a come back, eventually winning out through physical might. This narrative structure is so ingrained into our psyche that we automatically accept violent retribution as the only way to deal with bad guys—witness all the films and television shows which are underpinned by this idea. We accept tit-for-tat violence because we are conditioned to think that the good life will be, and can only be, achieved through the employment of retributive violence. (Of course, if everyone decides they are the good guys and that those they disagree with are the bad guys, then we have … today's world.)

From all this, we see that the warrior attitude so visible in sports, politics, business, entertainment, and religions can be interpreted as being both a continuation of those early Indo-European attitudes, and a manifestation of the concept of redemption through violence that continues to drive the modern era. Clearly, because humanity's current propensity to embrace confrontational warrior violence dates back at least five thousand years, and hence is deeply conditioned into us, it isn't going to disappear soon.

FREUD'S PERSPECTIVE

Sigmund Freud offered a different explanation for humanity's unease with itself, and its predisposition towards "ugly" behavior, in his theory of the ego, super-ego, and id.

Freud considered human beings are born with a number of subconscious, primitive, instinctual drives, which he identified with the id, and which manifest in the form of thirst, hunger and sex. He also considered that the id is propelled by the pleasure principle, which seeks immediate gratification of those drives. This means that if the id was let loose in society's living room, it would make a big mess on the carpet.

Each of us manage to function within socially prescribed norms because the ego, which is governed by the reality principle, contains the id's most destructive impulses, ensuring its drives are satisfied within socially acceptable bounds. Last to develop is the super-ego, which comprises our sense of morality and of right and wrong. It is conditioned into us by our parents and by the society we live in, and provides the ego with a wider social context in which to function.

For Freud, human beings are propelled by a number of powerful, primitive, self-centred drives (such as the warrior drive for dominance, territory, and status embodied in Indo-European culture), which are only kept in check by the ego inside us and by social strictures outside.

A biological corollary to Freud's three-part psychological model is offered by Paul MacLean in his triune model of the brain. MacLean's model suggests that the human brain consists of three distinct layers, which developed progressively as human beings evolved. These three layers are known as the R-complex or reptilian brain, the limbic system or proto-mammalian brain, and the neo-cortex or neo-mammalian brain.

The reptilian brain, like Freud's id, comprises sensory perception and our motor functions, along with our most primitive, instinctual drives; the proto-mammalian brain was developed by the earliest mammals, and encompasses emotions and memory, thus giving rise to identity and socializing factors; and the neo-mammalian brain comprises language and higher level thinking. MacLean's brain model thus again suggests that human beings have deep-seated instinctive urges that are held in check or channelled into more sophisticated behaviors by the two higher-level brains.

CONCLUSION

These ideas have taken us some distance from where we started with Augustine and his doctrine of original sin. However, we can see that behind Augustine's thought there is something worth considering—that humanity is a social animal, drawn to living in groups, yet living uneasily together.

The other thinkers examined have clarified our understanding of this easiness by giving us a picture of human behavior as consonant with that of a twenty-first century Indo-European warrior, living in a warring, conflict-riven age, driven by primitive instincts, whose social drives include violently obtaining possessions, territory, and status, and that these drives are barely held in check by social behavioral restrictions that result from conditioning by family members and the social environment.

What, then, can we take out of all this that is useful in relation to defining our moral yardstick? There is definitely something to consider in the repeated and uneasily asserted proposition that there is something is "wrong" with humanity. This is an issue we definitely have to take into account in our search for a moral yardstick by which to live.

However, for now I'll move on to consider moral codes.

CHAPTER 9

Morality As An Exercise In List-Making

We human beings have created numerous ethical and moral codes by which we live. Today these codes manifest in three principle forms: social norms, laws, and customs.

Social norms are what we consider normal. They are fundamental aspects of our social behavior that appear to be so valid and right that we don't question them. We then create laws and develop customs based on those norms. For example, if we considered it was normal for people to marry at the age of thirteen, then we would formulate laws and develop marriage customs based on that norm. If we later changed our mind, and decided sixteen or eighteen should be the age of marriage, then our laws would be rewritten to reflect this new idea of normal behavior.

Another example is slavery. Slavery became accepted in the Americas from the early 1600s, when labor was required in the newly established colonies. Customary relationships between owner and enslaved subsequently developed, and the legality of slavery was confirmed in various state law books in the late 1600s. A century later social norms changed, and it was agreed that slavery was no longer socially acceptable. Laws were enacted to reflect this new norm, laws which made slavery illegal in Portugal in 1761 and in England in 1772. In the USA this occurred in 1865, with the ratification of the 13th Amendment— although it wasn't until 1976 that the state of Kentucky, and in 1995 the state of Mississippi, added this Amendment to their law books.

Laws follow social norms, legitimizing (or de-legitimizing) behaviors in which citizens are already engaged. Further, what we consider to be "normal behavior" shapes the customs we develop and the social practices we carry out. However, what is of interest in all this is not any particular norm, law, or customary practice, but the idea behind them—that the moral codes we create for ourselves largely consist of lists of what is normal, what is legal, and what is customary.

We love to make lists. Lists clarify what we should think, say, or do. Lists show, in black and white, what is permitted and what is not permitted, what is good and which is bad.

Obviously, it would be extremely useful to our search for a moral yardstick if we could create such a list of ethical rules, slap the list on the table, and proclaim, "This list is our moral yardstick!"

Many of us yearn for the concrete, clear, and irrefutable knowledge we think such a list would provide. Why? Because morality would then become a very simple exercise of observing a person's behavior, comparing it to the items in the list, and approving of or condemning people on that basis. Even a child could understand it.

Unfortunately for this scenario, there is one small problem. Because the question that immediately arises is: Exactly which items should be on this list? As we have seen, much of our sense of what is right and wrong is not only so-cially determined, it is also shaped by self-interest. Thus a small-business person, a corporate lawyer, a sports-mad fan, a social philanthropist, a drug-dealer, a re-ligious worshipper, and a multi-national corporate manager, would each have very different suggestions as to what items should be on such a list, and the order of moral value for those items. Let's consider this issue in more detail.

RELIGION AS LIST-MAKING

The most famous list of rules Westerners have used to regulate their moral be-havior is the Ten Commandments. Yahweh supposedly carved his Command-ments in stone and gave them to Moses on Mt Sinai, around the same time Zarathushtra was herding cattle and inventing a new religion on the Iranian steppes. These Commandments are a list of seven "thou shalt nots" and three "thou shalts": thou shalt not murder, steal, commit adultery, bear false witness, covert thy neighbor's wife or goods, worship graven images, take God's name in vain; and thou shalt observe the Sabbath, honour your parents, and have no other God beside Yahweh.

The Jews were not alone in creating such a list. The Indian yoga teachings of Vedanta have a list of *yamas* (restraints). The yoga exponent Patanjali listed these in relation to the external world as non-killing, truthfulness, non-stealing, sexual discipline, and not receiving gifts. Other Indian texts list ten yamas, adding patience, steadfastness, compassion, moderation of appetites, and purity.[11]

Similarly, the Egyptian religion associated a moral code with Ma'at, the goddess who personified sacred order, morality, and justice. This moral code is listed in *The Forty-Two Declarations of Purity*, which were written on the walls of tombs to guide the newly-deceased in their passage into the next world. They included: I have not killed; I have not committed adultery or rape; I have not caused terror; I have not caused misery; I have not stolen; I have not lied; I have not spoken scornfully of others; I have not wasted running water; I have not hindered the flow of running water; I have not polluted the land; I have not judged any hastily or harshly; I have not acted proudly or with arrogance; I have not taken God's name in vain.[12] Clearly, several echo the Ten Commandments, which they preceded by hundreds of years.

Lists containing ethical rules and guidance for behavior are obviously useful, because they allow a society to agree on what is socially good and desirable, and draw an inarguable line between ethical and unethical behavior. The question is, do such lists still work today? Let's return to the list of rules provided by the Ten Commandments and ask: Is this a moral code by which we can usefully live?

The first thing that becomes apparent is that many of the Ten Commandments are irrelevant to today's Western secular world. When Moses brought the tablets down from Mt Sinai the Ten Commandments had religious significance and social relevance for the small tribal community in which he lived. Today Western culture is secular, so the Commandments may be religiously relevant to individuals, but they are not significant to Western nations as a whole. Further, our social structure is so different from that of the tribal peoples Moses led that most of the Ten Commandments have become irrelevant.

Consider the following: "Thou shalt have no graven image before Me"— we live in a world filled with audio-visual media in which images proliferate, and we worship famous entertainment and sports stars. "Thou shalt keep the Sabbath"—most Western countries are officially secular so have no God to keep the Sabbath for. "Thou shalt not commit adultery"—adultery is common among both sexes, marriage is no longer considered to be for life, divorce is easily obtained, and the prevailing form of sexual relationship is serial monogamy. "Thou shalt not steal"—governments, companies, and individuals in all colonized countries have taken lands from indigenous peoples, and the rich in all Western societies are getting much richer, much faster, than the middle and laboring classes. "Thou shalt not kill"—war proliferates, humanity as a whole kills thousands of people a day for various ideological and economic reasons, and religious leaders around the world endorse armies going to war.

From this it is clear that the Ten Commandments have little to contribute to our search for a moral yardstick. And, besides, how much do people conform to what is on lists anyway?

This question dates back to Moses, who found that having given his people the Ten Commandments, and despite it being given to them in the name of their God, his people proved incapable of keeping them. As a consequence Jewish prophets for centuries after Moses kept telling their people how angry God was with them for not keeping his Commandments, explaining that the bad things that kept happening to them were their punishment for being disobedient. So getting a nation to agree to a set of religiously-generated rules, then having them stick to them, has had its problems ever since the idea was first tried.

Clearly, all countries today have extensive rules listed on their legal statute books. The police, bureaucrats, and the courts exist to ensure that citizens obey them. However, most of these laws are concerned with property, ownership, and revenue gathering. A lesser number relate to normalized social practices such as marriage, sexual relationships, and the age at which citizens may start engaging in what are defined as adult activities, i.e. driving cars, voting, or drinking alcohol.

No one pretends that these lists of rules are anything but human-created. The reason we have laws today prohibiting theft and murder is not because Moses published them, but because we don't think murder and theft are good ways of living together. So these laws result from moral relativism.

However, for those who wish for some kind of objective scale of rules, the idea of a divinely-commanded or derived list of rules, a list that transcends human self-interest and limitations, still holds immense appeal. Why is this? I'll now examine in greater detail the nature of religiously-generated moral rules.

RELIGIONS AND REVELATORY EXPERIENCES

Religions have created innumerable lists of rules and regulations telling us what we can and can't do. We have already explored some of the implications—and limitations—of this tendency. What I will now do is examine this issue of rules from another angle, by looking at the way religions present doctrines and rules as intrinsic to their religious beliefs, yet they actually have nothing to do with the religion's founder's views.

For example, Jesus made no statements on the hierarchy of clergy, contraception, purgatory, or the resurrection of the body. But Christian churches have much to say about those topics. As we saw with the doctrine of original sin, embedded in religions are doctrines that are unrelated to, or even diverge from, their founder's original outlook. Further to this, Buddhism, Judaism, Islam, and the Vedic religions have all developed rules and regulations that add to or diverge from what is stated in their sacred texts, but that today are viewed by worshippers as having equal authority with their founder's original teachings.

This leads to the question of what religions are actually founded on. What is the reason religions come into existence? Zoroastrianism, Judaism, Buddhism, Christianity, and Islam came to be because highly spiritual individuals underwent a spiritually revelatory experience that was so powerful that they were compelled to share their insights. From the subsequent process of sharing a religion came into existence. This is true of all religions: their founders' revelatory experiences are at their heart. No revelation, no religion.

For example, Zarathushtra emphasized the importance of living the good life, in the here-and-now. But within the here-and-now he experienced a transcendent spiritual reality, which he called Ahura Mazda. Zarathushtra didn't refer much to his own experiences in his writings. Instead he sought to provide spiritual seekers with guidance so they could also experience what he had. As he put it in his *Gathas*:

> I have seen Ahura Mazda with my inner sight. … How shall I attain my ecstatic goal, guided by you, which is reaching Mazda [wisdom] and becoming one with him? … The person who desires inner light and tries to achieve it, O Mazda, do bestow it on him, through your holy and bright wisdom.[13]

Compared to Zarathushtra's reticence regarding his spiritual experiences, the circumstances that led to the Buddha's spiritual experiences are well known. After leaving his family, Gautama spent several years of apparently fruitless endeavour meditating and engaged in various austerities. Finally, he decided to sit under a peepul tree (a variety of fig), and not move until he had achieved enlightenment. After further struggle he experienced nirvana and came to understand the causes of suffering which had troubled him for so long. Tradition has it that the first words spoken by the Buddha after his enlightenment were:

> Through many a birth in samsara have I wandered in vain, seeking the builder of this house. Repeated birth is suffering! House-builder, you are seen! You will not build this house again. For your rafters are broken and your ridgepole shattered. My mind has reached the Unconditioned; I have attained the destruction of craving.[14]

This revelatory experience Buddha called nirvana. The experience of nirvana then became central to his teaching, the purpose of which, as with Zarathushtra, was to guide others so that they would eventually have an experience of nirvana themselves.

In the Judaic tradition, one of the most intriguing stories told of Moses is his experience of seeing God as a burning bush that is not consumed by flames (*Exodus* 3:1). That Moses saw God in this form (or, at least, described his experience using this image) suggests he considered that God's nature is beyond comprehension—exactly as is the case with a burning bush that remains unconsumed.

Obviously, seeing a burning bush is not an everyday experience. How did Moses come to experience it, or at least, to have an experience which he described in this way? The Kabbalah mystics consider Moses didn't just stumble onto a burning bush one day while strolling through the desert. Rather, it was a mystic experience that he achieved through ascetic disciplines. As the fourteenth century Rabbi Simon ben Tzemach Duran suggests about Moses:

> With his keen mind, he was able to understand what was required to attain enlightenment, realizing the path was through meditation. He therefore chose to separate himself from all who would disturb him and to reject all physical desires, choosing to be a shepherd in the desert, where no people are to be found. While he was there he unquestionably attained a great attachment to the conceptual, divesting himself of all bodily desires, until he was able to remain for forty days and forty nights without eating or drinking.[15]

From this we can see that Moses' spiritual authority derived from profound experiences. Similarly, Jesus Christ underwent a forty day fast in the desert, during which time he had spiritual experiences the depth of which the New Testament stories only hint at, and was so changed by those experiences that he started teaching immediately afterwards.

The Holy Prophet of Islam, Mohammed, also underwent a profound experience when an angel of God appeared to him, requiring him to transform his life. We can imagine a glowing angel dressed in white robes, maybe with wings. But such a description can only be a concrete, imaginable image for what, to Mohammed, must have been a profoundly exciting and disturbing experience that led to the founding of Islam. Spiritual experiences remained at the core of Mohammed's life, as is indicated in the story of his night time ascension into the heavens, a spiritual journey that non-canonical texts suggest Jesus also undertook, and that Jewish prophets experienced before them both. These transcendent experiences validated each of these founders' teachings in a practical way, showing their followers that a greater spiritual reality exists, and that it is ultimately attainable.

But if spiritually transcendent experiences exist at the heart of all religions, experiences that are variously associated with inner goodness (Zoroastrianism), inner freedom (Buddhism), knowing transcendence (Judaism), loving transcendence (Christianity), and peaceful surrender (Islam), why is it that religions spend so much time on rules, restrictions, taboos, and punishments that not only make millions feel bad about themselves, but that through their application end up creating misery, oppression, and hurt? Why is there such a gap between the inner transcendent experience that gave rise to each religion, and the constricting, oppressive rules and judgments that so religions project and protect?

A MODEL TO EXPLAIN WHY
RELIGIONS CREATE SO MANY RULES

A simple answer to this question is that after religious founders underwent their revelatory spiritual experiences, they were moved to guide others so they could achieve the same experiences for themselves. Over time, this guidance became established as a set of rules. Later still, other religious teachers gave their interpretations of these rules, adding layers of interpretation and exegesis, from which were derived even more rules. Eventually, the layers of rules and regulations become so thick and complex that priests and worshippers forgot about the transcendent experiences that lay at their religion's heart and focussed instead on the rules.

The following model is offered as a way of analyzing this process.It has eight descending steps. (See FIGURE 9.1)

1. Transcendent experience. The first step in the creation of religious rules is an experience of transcendent reality. Without there being such an experience religions would have no reason to exist. Human experience of transcendent reality provides us with the ultimate goal towards which human religion and spirituality strive.

2. Non-verbal communication. This step's non-verbal communication with respect to the first step's transcendent spiritual experience. Many times Buddha remained silent when asked abstract or metaphysical questions. In one famous incident he held up a flower in answer to a question. In another he was asked if there was a spiritual self. When he remained silent his questioner asked if that meant he agreed there was no spiritual self. Again Buddha remained silent. The only complete answer to such a question, of course, is for the questioner to experience spiritual reality and so find out directly for him or her self.

3. Verbal teaching. The third step provides for those who are unable to understand non-verbal guidance. The Buddha spent forty years teaching tens of thousands of people, outlining what he considered they needed to do in order to to achieve such an experience for themselves. Similarly, Jesus spent three years travelling and teaching, Mohammed offered extensive verbal guidance, which were collected into his *hadith*, and Zarathushtra spent years discussing, cajoling, and convincing others. In effect, the aim of this third step is to provide a stepping-stone to prepare followers for non-verbal guidance and to lay the groundwork for their own experience of transcendent spiritual reality.

First deflection. What distinguishes these first three steps is that they all involve direct interaction with the religion's founder. This means that on all these three steps the goal of transcendent spiritual experience remains a living possibility in all communication. But then the founder dies, and followers are left to carry on by themselves. This creates a huge gap between new followers and the founder's original transcendent experience, a gap incorporated in the model as the first deflection. Those who knew the founder personally are generally happy to continue on their way, remembering what they have been taught and knowing what they have to do. But for later generations of followers, who lack this direct personal contact, there rises a desire to have access to the founder's teachings. A need for a permanent written record then develops. Thus we reach the fourth step.

4. Creation of primary texts. At this stage a rudimentary biography is constructed, and the first written forms of the teaching are collected, or written, if the founder left no texts of his own. Zarathushtra wrote his own texts, putting his teaching's central concepts, along with references to key life events, into his *Gathas*. However, a vast literature was added over the centuries to this initial small record, with the vast majority of Zoroastrian sacred texts well and truly post-dating Zarathushtra.

In the case of Judaism, Abraham left no texts, and while the Penteuch has Moses' name attached to it, it is unlikely that he wrote any of these texts given that he lived around 1,200 BCE and inter-textural evidence suggests the texts date to around 600 BCE. In the case of Buddhism, the Buddha also left no written record of his teachings. However, oral forms of his teachings circulated for centuries, until the decision was made to collect them in written form around 200 BCE. Jesus similarly left no written record. The four *Gospels* contain details of his life and teachings, although there is much dispute regarding which biographical details are correct, and which sayings might be those that Jesus actually spoke. This is made even more complex by the fact that Jesus and his disciples spoke Aramaic, whereas the Gospels were written in Greek. In the case of Islam Mohammed was illiterate, so others wrote down the teaching he was given, often on scraps of cloth or skin. Mohammed never oversaw the editing of all those various scraps of writing, with the *Qur'an* only being collated a hundred years after Mohammed had passed on.

This post-founder process of gathering, writing, selecting, and editing sacred texts inevitably involves a process of accretion, in which mythological and miraculous elements are added to the biography, and interpretations, interpolations, and extrapolations are added to the founder's remembered—or perhaps not so well-remembered—words.

This stage also gives rise to an interesting shift. In the first three steps the founder's transcendent experience was the ultimate focus of all non-verbal guidance and verbal teaching. But with the creation of sacred texts a new focus is on offer: the sacred texts themselves. Thus followers' attention shifts from contemplating the higher goal of experiencing transcendent reality for themselves, to the lower goal of appreciating the sacred text. A sacred text rapidly develops its own existence independent of the founder, with followers busying themselves remembering, interpreting, and putting into practice the words of their sacred texts. Because many followers don't understand these words—historically many couldn't even read—there then also arises a need for authorities to interpret the texts for others. The texts then become the fulcrum around which a religion forms. And the fourth step, rather than the first, becomes the religion's focus..

5. *Codification.* This brings us to the fifth step, which involves the codification of the founder's teachings and practices. This process usually takes several centuries to develop. It arises because later generations of followers wish to understand the intricacies of all the founder taught, so they make extensive use of the interpretations offered by later religious authorities. As disagreements over interpretation occur, schisms develop, and break-away sects form. This step is not necessarily negative, because at this stage the teaching may also be adjusted to ensure it remains relevant to changing social, intellectual, cultural, and religious requirements and needs. In fact, the shock of the religion

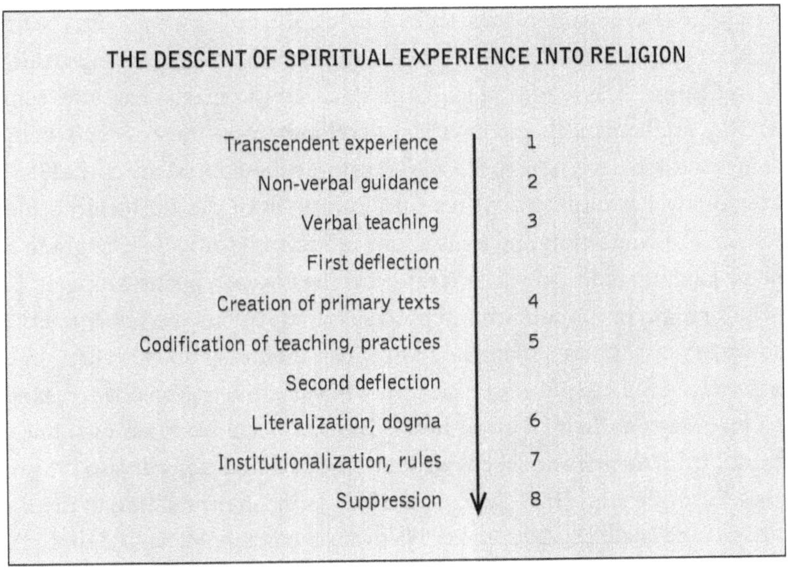

THE DESCENT OF SPIRITUAL EXPERIENCE INTO RELIGION

Transcendent experience	1
Non-verbal guidance	2
Verbal teaching	3
First deflection	
Creation of primary texts	4
Codification of teaching, practices	5
Second deflection	
Literalization, dogma	6
Institutionalization, rules	7
Suppression	8

FIGURE 9.1

coming into contact with other traditions, and religious authorities having to justify their religion in the face of the conceptual or spiritual challenge offered by other scholars and authorities, can have fascinating and highly influential results.

For example, the Greek city of Alexandria, established in Egypt around 331 BCE, was a key Mediterranean port, drawing traders from as far away as India, Anatolia, Central Asia, Africa, Rome, Greece, and France. It also brought the rabbis of Judaism in contact with Greek philosophy, which contact gave rise to the Jewish Wisdom literature, led to the development of Gnostic spirituality, and provided the environment for a thinker such as Philo to blossom. Philo interpreted Jewish religious texts using Greek allegorical methods, and merged the abstract First Cause of Greek philosophy with the personal god Yahweh of Judaic religion.[16] This was also the period when Jewish Talmudic mystic schools first came to prominence, laying the groundwork for the teachings of Kabbalah.[17]

The same process occurred in Islam. After Mohammed passed on, the caliphs of Islam embarked on a series of conquests, including of Alexandria. The immediate result was that numerous manuscripts were brought back to Islamic scholars in Baghdad and Damascus. These scholars then came face to face with Greek philosophy, mathematics, logic, politics, and biology, and with the mystical Neoplatonism that had developed seven hundred years earlier in Alexandria and Rome. This exposure led Islamic scholars to make great intellectual, scientific, mathematical, and mystical developments—the concepts behind Sufi mysticism derive, in part, from Neoplatonic thought. Many of these ideas subsequently started filtering back into Europe from the thirteenth century when Greek manuscripts and translations of ancient texts were brought to Europe by Islamic traders and scholars fleeing the invasion by the Mongols.[18]

The strength of the codification process is that it offers the opportunity for followers to re-appraise the direction in which their religion is headed, and to turn it away from religious texts and back towards the transcendental experience that exists at their religion's heart. This has occurred at various times in Judaism, Christianity, and Islam, via their mystical traditions. It also occurred in Buddhism, around 100 CE, when the Mahayana interpretation of the Buddha's teaching challenged the earlier Hinayana approach. Mahayana shifted the emphasis from the earlier narrow, rational, and historical view, to an intuitive, personal, transformative, enlightenment-focused outlook. Where in Hinayana only the Buddha was called a *bodhisattva* (seeker of enlightenment), in Mahayana all spiritual seekers were called *bodhisattvas*, and all shared the same goal of achieving the Buddha's experience of nirvana.[19]

Second deflection. However, during the process of codification the opposite may also occur, closing down the spiritual possibilities of followers by taking their religion further away from direct spiritual experience. In the last three steps a religion becomes increasingly inward-looking, overly concerned with its own governance, status and rules, and focused on the observance of religious strictures instead of the strivings of followers to achieve transcendent spiritual experiences.

6. *Literalization.* The first of these final three steps involves literalization and dogma. By literalization is meant ignoring the symbolic nature of the language used in sacred texts, and instead interpreting symbols and metaphors as literal truths. Dogma builds theological arguments and statements on literal interpretations.

In Christianity, this sixth step occurred at the Council of Nicea, which formalized the dogma of Jesus Christ being the actual son of God, "co-substantial with the Father, begotten and not created", and asserted that Jesus ascended bodily into heaven. Over the centuries, there has been significant theological debate among Christians regarding the degree to which texts should be interpreted literally, and if interpreted symbolically, what interpretations are permissible. Sufi and Christian mystics who at interpreted texts from a mystical perspective were at times declared heretics, which resulted in them being persecuted, imprisoned and occasionally put to death by violent defenders of the orthodoxy. Indeed, the formalization of dogma in any religion is largely made on the assumption that the experiences of the founder are unavailable to believers, and so the dogmatic position becomes that believers should limit themselves to studying the sacred texts, and to interpreting those texts according to orthodox teaching.

7. *Institutionalization.* The seventh step, which involves institutionalization and the establishment of rules, is even further from the founder's experience. Few, or perhaps none, of these rules were originally stated by the founder. Instead, they are rules religious authorities have created to uphold the institution. For example, the Catholic Church has numerous rules that define what a sin is, the degrees of sinfulness, and what the penance is for each one. All religions, even Judaism and the many Hindu sects, which are not institutional

in the Christian sense, have innumerable rules governing followers' religious and social behavior, along with extensive interpretative texts outlining what is and what is not permitted. The Buddha did foresee the need for certain rules by which the *sangha* (monastic assembly) could govern itself. However, he never envisioned Buddhism becoming an institution—or that he himself would be worshipped as divine.

8. Oppression and suppression. Finally, we move down to the eighth step, outright oppression and suppression. This is where people use religious dogmas and rules to oppress and exploit others, both inside their own religion and socially. Religious oppression has created immense misery. As this has been extensively documented through the centuries, there is no need to discuss this eighth step further here.

SUMMARY

What is being suggested here is that the more rigid a religion becomes, the more inward-looking and involved in its own internal processes, the further it moves from the founder's original revelatory experience. Thus, as a religion replaces transcendent experience with sacred texts, literalizes the interpretation of those texts, and generates lists of rules based on that interpretation, the further it leads followers away from the spirituality that provided the reason for the religion to come into existence in the first place.

Of course, this does not mean that religions are *only* mechanisms of dogma and repression, because individual seekers still retain the possibility of rising above low-aiming literal dogma and reaching the deeper experiences and understanding that is at the core of their religion.

I will examine this possibility shortly. In the meantime, I'll continue examining implications of the religious moral objectivist view.

CHAPTER 10

Conscience And The Afterlife

Two other key ideas behind the moral objectivist view feed into and shape our concepts of morality. These are, firstly, our actions in this life being rewarded or punished in the next, and, secondly, the impact of conscience. I'll start with the afterlife.

We are all familiar with the idea that if we are good or bad during our lives, our actions will be rewarded or punished in the afterlife. This is meant to provide us with a strong motive for being good in this one. There are two aspects to this belief. One is the idea that after our body dies we, as individuals, continue to exist in spiritual form, and that as a spirit we undergo a moral judgment of the actions we carried out while alive on Earth. The second aspect is that there will be an end to time, and that the world as a whole will be judged. Where do these ideas come from?

ANCIENT CONCEPTS OF THE AFTERLIFE

The ancient Egyptians believed that after their body's death they entered the Hall of Double Truth and Right, where the process of Weighing of the Heart was carried out. In some versions of this Weighing the process involves the Heart being placed in one scale and the rest of the person in the other scale. The process was overseen by the gods Ma'at and Thoth.

The goddess Ma'at was similar to the Zoroastrian asha. She represented the principles of order, truth, and justice. Thoth mediated between humanity and the gods. It was his task to record the result of the Weighing of the Heart and to pass it on to the other gods. The Egyptians saw the Heart as always pure, because it had its home in Ma'at and so could never be defiled. The Heart being weighed against the rest of the person was a symbolic way of representing whether the dead had achieved a balance between their deepest spiritual part on the one hand and all the psychological, psychic, and physical aspects of their being on the other. A prayer indicated what this process meant to Egyptians:

> My heart, my mother!
> O my heart of my time upon earth!
> May nothing stand up to oppose me in judgment
> In the presence of the Keeper of the Balance.
> Let it not be said of me or of what I have done:
> "He has done things against Ma'at."[20]

Philosopher and cultural historian Jeremy Naydler has drawn attention to how, in the *Papyrus of Hunefer* (drawn around 1,200 BCE, the time of both Zarathushtra and Moses) two possible post-death outcomes are shown. If the Weighing of the Heart of the newly dead Hunefer results in an acceptable outcome, Horus is there to lead Hunefer off to meet Osirus (the God of rebirth) in the Underworld. But if the weighing has an unacceptable outcome, the dog-shaped Ammit was present to devour Hunefer and his Heart on the spot.[21]

Zarathushtra also considered there was a spiritual and moral weighing after death. He drew on ancient Iranian mythology to suggest the testing place was the Chivat Bridge. Zarathushtra proposed that the newly dead person arrived at this bridge where his or her thoughts, words, and deeds were appraised, a judgment was made, and reward or punishment ensued.

> The Inner Self of the wicked man destroys the reality of the straight way. His soul shall surely vex him at the Chivat Bridge. ... This I ask, Lord. What punishment shall be for him who promotes the power of a wicked man? For him who finds no other means of livelihood than harming the cattle and men of the honest pastor? ... A long life of darkness, foul food, the crying of woe—to that existence, o wicked ones, your Inner Self shall lead you. ... [On the other hand] Lord Mazda will give perpetuity of communion with Good Purpose to him who is His ally in spirit and acts.[22]

This quotation from Zarathushtra's *Gathas* presents the idea of a Last Judgment at the end of time, a concept that subsequently influenced Judaic, Christian, and Islamic ideas regarding the afterlife and moral judgment. Interestingly, the Zoroastrian Last Judgment considers that at the end of time both the good and the evil will be purged for three days—the evil in molten metal—then both groups will together join Ahura Mazda in his kingdom for eternity.[23]

The Buddha, like Zarathushtra and the Egyptians, considered morality was fundamental to following his teaching. His Eightfold Noble Path divided into three parts: morality, meditation, and wisdom. Morality involves right speech, right actions, and right livelihood. The Buddha considered these three laid the foundations for all subsequent spiritual enquiry and development; without this moral basis Buddhist seekers could not develop spiritually. Thus morality laid the platform for transcendent spiritual experiences. This agrees with the outlooks of Zoroastrianism, Judaism, Christianity, Islam, and the ancient Egyptian religion. However, Buddhism also added a belief in reincarnation.

REINCARNATION AND MORALITY

Western religions take the view that we have one life, with one roll of the moral dice, and that after that one roll we have eternity to face the consequences. In contrast, the view of Dharmic religions—Jainism, the post-Vedic religions, and Buddhism—is that we do not have just one shot at getting our life right morally, we actually have many rolls of the dice. In life after life we are reborn into new bodies, which results in our having multiple opportunities to refine our moral perspective, to "do the right thing," and to grow from a self-involved to an expansive outlook.

The cycle of births and deaths was termed *samsara* by Buddha. As outlined earlier, the spiritual aim in Buddhism is to enter the state of nirvana and escape the cycle of births and deaths, for nirvana is not just a transcendental spiritual experience that is attained in this life, but is also the afterlife state the enlightened enter subsequent to the body's death. Thus where the metaphysical goal of Abrahamic religions is to enter a heavenly paradise (and avoid going to the hellish other place), freedom is the goal for Buddhism and the other Dharmic religions. (Hell is considered to be life on Earth.) However, Eastern and Western religions share the belief that entering a heavenly paradise or a state of inner freedom depends on living a morally good life.

Plato's philosophy has not been mentioned in this discussion of religious beliefs because Platonic thought is not a religion. But it is interesting to consider that where Western religions all believe in only one life, Plato shared with the Indian Dharmic religions a belief in reincarnation. And he was not the only Greek philosopher who thought this. While the Greek religion, as it was practiced by the general populace, believed that human beings have one life in this world then go on to the afterlife, a number of Greek and Roman philosophers accepted the doctrine of reincarnation. These philosophers included Pythagoras, Pherecydes, Parmenides, Empedocles, Aristotle, Plutarch, Proclus, and Plotinus.[24] Indeed, the idea of reincarnation was not only accepted by Aristotle, but he considered Plato to be the reincarnation of Zarathushtra!

The Greek and Indian philosophers also shared the same view of what reincarnation entailed, which consisted of: (1) the process of incarnation (Sanskrit *samsara*, Greek *metempsychosis*), (2) moral and cognitive laws governing the process (Sanskrit *karma*, Greek *katharsis*), (3) the goal of escaping from repeated reincarnations (Sanskrit *moksa*, Greek *lusis*).'[25]

The concept of karma underpins reincarnation. Initially karma referred to the merit (or demerit) people accumulated during their lifetimes as a result of their actions. After the body's death, people went to a heavenly or hellish place where they used up the karma they had accumulated. Then, when that karma ran out, they were reborn into another body. As the *Bhagavad Gita* puts it:

> Who follow the three Vedas, drink juice
> of soma to purge themselves of sin, and offer
> sacrifices in worship, seek the abode of heaven;
> in reward, they reach the realm of the gods,
> in heaven tasting the gods' divine joys.
> That vast realm enjoyed, and all merit spent,
> they then return to the world of mortals.[26]

From around 700 BCE, a new view of karma and rebirth developed. Presented in the Upanishads, the ancient Indian philosophic and mystic texts, karma and reincarnation became linked in a more complex psycho-spiritual relationship. For them there was no heaven or hell that people went to after death. Instead, people were incarnated in another body, and the karma they had accumulated during their lifetime influenced what situation they were born into in their next life. These Upanishad mystics viewed karma is a moral mechanism by which we choose our own future rewards and punishments through our own actions. The Greek philosophers understood reincarnation in exactly the same sense. As noted by Thomas McEvilley, a scholar who has thoroughly examined the ideas of both Greek and Indian philosophers in this matter:

> According to the form of the doctrine that is found in both Greece and India … it is the moral quality of one's past behavior that determines the type of rebirth one will have. Plato, for example, says (*Laws* X.903d) that the process of kartharsis—purification through successive reincarnations—shifts "the character that is becoming better to a better incarnation, and that which is growing worse to a worser, each according to its due." The *Chandogya Upanisad* (V.10.7) similarly says: "Those whose conduct here has been good will quickly attain a good birth … but those whose conduct here has been evil will quickly attain an evil birth." Plato and the Upanisadic teacher may mean different things by good, but in any case the idea of karmic accumulation with positive-negative polarity is in effect in both texts.[27]

Plainly, then, whether one adopts a traditional Western religious "one roll of the moral dice" scenario, or an Eastern and Greek philosophic "multiple rolls" view, the same weighing of the moral qualities of our lives applies. In addition, all share the view that not only all our thoughts, words, and deeds count, in Zarathushtra's words, our "inner self" is also weighed.

We can draw from these metaphysical ideas that morality doesn't just involve how we treat others, it also involves what we are inside ourselves. The state of our inner self is therefore as important as our outer actions in defining ourselves as moral beings. Indeed, from the religious and philosophic perspectives, our inner self is more important, because our internal thoughts, feelings, and intentions influence what we do and say in the exterior world.

From this, it can now be said that the moral yardstick we are seeking has to function both externally, in relation to others in the communities in which we live, and internally, in relation to our psychological states.

CONSCIENCE

This brings us to the issue of conscience. It could be asked why are we devoting so much space to looking for a moral yardstick when we are born with a ready-made yardstick—our conscience. As long as we obey our conscience, we will always be doing right. But what, exactly, is conscience?

"Conscience" is one of the words we most commonly use in relation to moral choice, as is seen in statements such as, "It's against my conscience," or "So-and-so has no conscience," or "That will play on my conscience." Yet while it is a word we use frequently, how it works in us is not as clear.

Most of us would say that conscience is an inner sense or feeling we have regarding what is right or wrong to do. Conscience performs a preventative role in our lives when it makes us feel morally uncomfortable about carrying out an action and holds us back from performing it, as with conscientious objectors who refuse to go to war. Conscience can also provide us with an initiating role, in situations where we feel compelled to act on our conscience, such as becoming a corporate whistle-blower, or protesting against animal testing or to support environmental issues. Conscience also provides instant certitude when we are evaluating situations that require a moral perspective, giving us a handy "straight off-the-rack" inner certainty of what is right and what is wrong. Preventing, initiating, and providing instant certitude—these are the three ways conscience functions inside us.

But where does this certitude actually come from? From our head? Our heart? Our soul? From God? Or is our sense of right and wrong actually shaped by external influences? For instance, by sacred texts? By what our church leaders say? By what our parents or friends say? Is conscience innate or conditioned? Is conscience even a "thing" at all?

By way of finding a starting point, let's go back to Peter Singer and see what he has to say from a secular, morally objective viewpoint. Interestingly, he has a problem with the idea that conscience is an innate, instinctive sense that we can draw on for a moral evaluation without thought or rational engagement:

> When "following conscience" means doing as one's "inner voice" prompts one to do, to follow one's conscience is to abdicate one's responsibility as a rational agent, to fail to take all the relevant factors into account and act on one's best judgment of the rights and wrongs of the situation. The "internal voice" is more likely to be a product of one's upbringing and education than a source of genuine ethical insight.[28]

Peter Singer is making two points here. The first is that morality is a process that occurs using rational thought. This suggests that conscience, too, should be part of a rational process of decision-making. Singer's second point is that any "inner voice" that we hear is created in us by upbringing and education. This means that if we associate conscience with an inner voice, then not only does conscience have no higher provenance, it is in fact nothing more than an echo of what others feed into us.

Other thinkers echo Singer's thoughts on the way our sense of right and wrong is constructed, which requires further consideration. Accordingly, I'll conduct a brief survey of how conscience is viewed from the psychological, social, biological, and religious perspectives, starting with that of Freud.

THE FREUDIAN PERSPECTIVE

Freud argued that we possess three fundamental psychological parts: id, ego, and super-ego. The id is the wild part of us that is full of irrational and instinctive desires. The super-ego is the internalization of what societies consider to be acceptable behavior. It opposes the id's irrational desires. The levers societies use to keep their citizens' ids under control consist of social norms, communal rules, national laws, and customs. The ego stands midway between the id and the super-ego, mediating between our irrational desires and the restrictions placed on our desires by our society.

According to Freud's model, conscience cannot be innate because our only inner voice is that of the irrational id. I noted earlier that in general terms we consider conscience to be an inhibitor of our actions, a feeling or inner voice that provides us with certainty about what is right and wrong. Freud considered that because society provides the major inhibitors on our behavior, conscience is part of the super-ego. Our conscience is created by the rules that we internalize during the process of growing up and becoming socialized.

Freud's view, then, is that conscience is an internalization of social levers that society has created in order to control its citizens' iraational desires. We may experience onscience as an inner voice, but the things that voice says, the assumptions that underpin it, are absorbed by us from the wider community. So conscience is really a social construct.

THE NEO-EVOLUTIONARY PERSPECTIVE

The new evolutionary thinkers take a very different tack to Freud. Yet, interestingly, Darwin's own thoughts on conscience arguably stood closer to those of

Freud than to those of his followers today. For Darwin, conscience was allied to a socialized moral sense. He wrote that conscience is:

> Ultimately a highly complex sentiment, having its first origin in the social instincts, largely guided by the approbation of our fellow men, ruled by reason, self-interest, and in later times by deep religious feelings, confirmed by instruction and habit, all combined, constitute our moral sense or conscience.[29]

Darwin held that religious feelings were among the most sophisticated of our responses. They combine with self-interest and reason to create moral sensibility. So for Darwin, as for Freud, conscience arises from a negotiation between what we want and what the social environment will allow.

Darwin's view of conscience could be seen as a strategy we adopt to adjust our individual behavior to social precepts. For today's leading evolutionary thinkers, strategizing is a key to conscience. But the strategies they envisage encompass a much greater range of behaviors than those envisaged by Darwin, who lived in a pre-Freudian world in which the power of subconscious impulses was not understood as it is today. However, for evolutionary thinkers, these impulses emanate not from the id, but from the genes.

In their approach to conscience, today's evolutionary thinkers place more emphasis on internal, unconscious processes than on the processes of socialization—although, obviously, our behavior is a socialized manifestation of those inner impulses. Scientist Steven Pinker has drawn attention to the work of an anthropologist, Richard Shweder, and that of psychologist Jonathan Haidt to formulate an evolutionary perspective on morality that brings together the genetic and social levels of our behavior.

Shweder has identified three fundamental spheres of group morality. These are the ethic of autonomy, the ethic of community, and the ethic of divinity.

> The ethic of autonomy pertains to an individual's interests and rights. It emphasizes fairness as the cardinal virtue, and is the cause of morality as it is understood by secular educated people in Western societies. The ethic of community pertains to the mores of the social group; it includes values like duty, respect, adherence to convention, and deference to a hierarchy. The ethic of divinity pertains to a sense of exalted purity and holiness, which is opposed to a sense of contamination and defilement.[30]

These three spheres encompass individual desires and interests, the social environment, and our feelings of transcendence. While, for Shweder, a sense of fairness is the touchstone that unites all three social spheres of our moral activity it is clear the are all forms of moral relativism, because each has a basis in social mores and socialized behavior.

In contrast, Haidt sees conscience as a behavioral strategy that ultimately emanates from our genes. These strategies are categorized as kin selection (we favor our own family members over other people), familial love (love reinforces family members' support for each other), reciprocal altruism (we help others when they need it so they will help us in the future when we need it), and the punishment of cheaters (we punish those who do not help us after we have helped them). The sole purpose behind these four strategies is to ensure our genes survive and replicate—because the evolutionary view is that human beings are no more than vehicles for carrying around genes.

Using these four strategies, Haidt proposes that there are that four groups of emotions. These four groups are: other-condemning emotions, which consist of contempt, anger and disgust, which we use to punish cheaters; the other-praising emotions, consisting of gratitude, and an elevating emotion that could be called moral awe or being moved, which we use to reward altruists; the oth-

	HAIDT'S FOUR MORAL EMOTIONS			
SHWEDER'S THREE SPHERES	Other-Condemning	Other-praising	Other-suffering	Self-conscious
Ethic of autonomy Personal rights, interests	Anger	Gratitude	Empathy	Guilt
Ethic of community Social values, mores	Contempt	Public honor	Sympathy	Embarrassment
Ethic of divinity Purity, defilement	Disgust	Awe	Compassion	Shame
	(Punish cheaters)	(Reward altruists)	(Help others)	(Avoid cheating)

FIGURE 10.1

er-suffering emotions, which consist of sympathy, compassion and empathy, which prompt us to help others; and the self-conscious emotions, consisting of guilt, shame, and embarrassment, which push us to avoid cheating others, and that we project onto others who cheat.[31] Further, Haidt suggests that Shweder's three spheres of group morality may also be interpreted as genetic survival strategies:

> Anger, for example, which is the other-condemning emotion in the sphere of autonomy, evolved from systems for aggression and was recruited to implement the cheater-punishment strategy demanded by reciprocal altruism. Disgust, the other-condemning emotion in the sphere of divinity, evolved from a system for avoiding biological contaminants like disease and spoilage. ... Embarrassment, the self-conscious emotion in the sphere of community, is a dead ringer for the gestures of appeasement and submission found in other primates.[32]

Where other thinkers consider that conscience is a social construct, or a religiously-dictated impulse, or a higher force inside us, the evolutionary view advocated by Haidt is that morality and conscience are survival strategies that operate at a biological level deep inside us, without our awareness, and even without our conscious participation. We are not moral. Rather, our genes "do" morality by dictating our social behavior. To paraphrase a well-known refrain: "It is an inner voice, Jim, but not as we know it."

THE PERSPECTIVE OF NEUROSCIENCE

Recent discoveries by neuroscientists further endorse the evolutionary perspective. Experimental evidence suggests that particular parts of the brain become active when certain moral questions are being addressed.

As noted earlier, the brain has three strata: the reptilian brain stem, the mammalian limbic brain, and the cerebral cortex. Together, these give us the ability to make the complex responses that are involved in moral decision-making.

Research by neuroscientists currently focuses on three areas: moral emotions, theory of mind, and abstract moral reasoning. Moral emotions are driven by the brain stem, and includes basic drives such as for food and sex. Theory of mind refers to the way we assess other's responses to us, so we can adjust our behavior to them. Abstract moral reasoning occurs throughout the brain, and involves the complex ways that we process information and transform it into moral decision-making. What unites all three is that they are all considered to be a function of brain activity and to be impacted by evolutionary selection.

Neuroscientist Michael S. Gazzaniga suggests, "altruistic instincts have been selected over time."[34] By this he means that a moral concern for others has become prevalent in human beings because we need each other in order to survive and reproduce. Over time more people who helped one another survived than those who did not. This resulted in people with an altruistic tendency initially outnumbering, then overwhelming, those who had no embedded altruistic tendency. In this way an altruistic tendency became selected over time.

Neuroscience is a rapidly evolving field of study, with many more discoveries yet to be made regarding the brain's functions and the way it impacts on our behavior. However, one of Gazzaniga's conclusions is illuminating in relation to our search for a moral yardstick:

> The new brain imaging results are highly suggestive that our brains are responding to the great underlying moral dilemmas. It is as if all the social data of the moment, the personal survival interests we each possess, the cultural experience we have undergone, and the basic temperament of our species, feed into the subconscious mechanisms we all possess and out comes a response, an urging for either action or inaction.[35]

Gazzaniga's conclusion suggests that morality exists due to the interaction of inner subconscious urges, our responses to our immediate environment, and the behavioral filters that we inherit genetically.

This brings us back to Freud's and Darwin's ideas on conscience: that conscience arises from a combination of subconscious urges, the accommodations we make in relation to our social environment, and the rational and non-rational processes which we use to make decisions. We like to think that we make decisions rationally, but as Freud and others have pointed out, in reality instinctive and tendencies behaviors play a huge part in whatever we decide.

THOMAS AQUINAS' PERSPECTIVE

Thomas Aquinas concluded that conscience is "not a special power or presence."[36] Conscience is not something that comes to us from God, nor is it a thing that exists in us. Instead, he argued that conscience is a process, in which we use our intelligence to weigh up situations and options, which we then act on. However, all this is mitigated by making reference back to the Christian moral code as its frame of reference, with Christ's dictum of "loving your neighbor as yourself" being the highest moral principle.

For Aquinas, conscience is the practical process of deciding what is the morally right thing to do. In deciding we use our powers of rational thought, which Aquinas also called practical reason, because its outcome is to decide what to do in a practical sense in the world. However, of ability to think rationally is a result of natural law.

Aquinas identified three principle levels of laws. The highest law is the eternal law, which is the idea God had before he created the universe. This idea was to do with the well-ordered functioning of the universe God subsequently created. The next level down is natural law, which is eternal law as it is embedded in the natural world, in the nature of each created being. For human beings, practical reason is fundamental to our nature. So God's eternal law dictates that we are naturally inclined towards reason, and to use our reason to understand God's eternal laws and our will to act in harmony with the eternal law. The lowest level is that of human laws, which ideally should be enacted out of a regard for both the higher natural and eternal laws.

By virtue of the eternal law manifesting in our nature we possess practical reason to decide what is the best action, and free will to act on the basis of what we decide. Aquinas calls the activity of making correct decisions prudence. So conscience involves the use of practical reason and free will to choose prudently.

CONSCIENCE AS A PROCESS

The difference between Aquinas' religious view of conscience, and those of the secular psychological, social, and biological thinkers I have just examined, is not as great as might be expected. All agree that *conscience is not an object, but a process.*

Of course, they do not agree on the level at which conscience occurs in us. For Freud it occurs in the super-ego as part of an inhibiting process by which we mediate our drives and desires to conform with society's regulations and rules. For evolutionary thinkers conscience derives from the unconscious strategies of our genes to survive and reproduce. For neuroscientists the brain is hardwired for decision-making, with the added suggestion that altruism is a behavior that has been selected over time. For religious thinkers such as Aquinas, conscience is a function of our using reason, but while decisions are rational, they are also made in the context of eternal laws, and in consideration of moral codes delivered to us via supernatural revelation.

From this we can derive three levels at which conscience is considered to function. These are: the biological level, of genes and our biological hardwiring, which includes instinctive impulses; the psychological level, of conditioned and inherited impulses, including both unconscious and consciously applied thinking, emotions and attitudes; the social level, in which we are pressured by those in our social environment to conform to social norms and rules; and the rational level, in which we think through the situation and its various aspects. While most religious and some philosophic thinkers consider there is a transcendental aspect to our morality, in the sense that they consider moral concepts and the impulse to be to come from a source that transcends the natural world, the process of moral decision-making that is our conscience remains firmly in this world, so the transcendent level may be ignored in this context. An additional consideration is that these three levels involve us in various degrees of participation.

At the biological level we have no conscious participation. Whether we consider our behavior from a Freudian or evolutionary perspective, either our id or our genes are making decisions entirely to satisfy their innate urges through unthinking biological processes of animal desire or natural selection, and human being are only along for the ride.

At the psychological level we have a range of participation, depending on how conscious we are of the impulses, thoughts, and emotions that affect our decision-making process. We know how much psychological tendencies and attitudes, such as prejudices, blind hope, greed, having a victim mentality, and pessimism or optimism affect our decision-making. Often we have external social and family pressures which push us to make certain decisions others desire. And part of the maturity process as human beings involves acquiring greater insight into how we and others make decisions so that we become aware of what exactly all the various inner impulses and external forces are that impact on our decision-making.

The rational level of decision-making assumes that we are able to make decisions that are derived entirely from a self-reflective process. This assumes that we can set aside or rise above those biological, psychological and social impulses and forces, including gut reactions and feelings of "rightness" that impact so hugely on our decision-making in other parts of our lives. Is this possible? If so, how does it work?

RATIONALITY AND MORAL DECISION-MAKING

I'll start enquiring into this issue with the thoughts of ethical philosopher, Peter Singer. For Singer, rational thought is necessary to moral decision-making, because without it we are not making moral decisions at all, we are doing no more than deciding on the basic of subconsciously functioning "gut" reactions.

Singer agrees with the new evolutionary thinkers that our moral sense has been shaped by the evolutionary mechanisms of kinship, reciprocal altruism, and empathy with others. However, he sees reason as adding something higher to humanity's evolutionary development, arguing that reason, while evolving in us as part of nature, offers us advantages that are beyond the specifically biological and social:

THREE APPROACHES TO CONSCIENCE AS A PROCESS			
	AQUINAS	NEO-DARWINIST	SINGER
WIDEST CONTEXT	God's eternal law	Biological hardwiring	Humanity and biosphere
DECISION PROCESS	Application of practical reason	Unconscious strategies emanating from genes	Rational thought
IMPETUS	Apply free will to do good	Naturally selected altruism	Universalize self-interest
AIM	Prudently decide what is right	Survive and reproduce	Make best decisions for all involved

FIGURE 10.2

> The ability to reason gives very general advantages. It does have important social aspects—it helps us to communicate better with others of our species, and hence to cooperate in more detailed plans ... [but] though a capacity to reason helps us survive and reproduce, once we develop a capacity for reasoning, we may be led by it to places that are not of any direct advantage to us, in evolutionary terms. Reason is like an escalator—once we step on it, we cannot get off until we have gone where it takes us.[36]

Singer is suggesting that the same evolutionary forces that led to us to develop an intellect capable of rational thought have also set in motion a natural process by which we can transcend the conditions by which evolution has defined us. Singer's suggestion leads to the idea that an evolution approach can take our thinking in two directions, one reductive, the other transcendent.

The first is the reductive direction suggested by Neo-Darwinian thinkers such as Richard Hawkins, Stephen Pinker, and Robert Wright, who argue that all our complex moral behavior is the result of our genes' blind, unconscious, unthinking quest to survive and reproduce.

The second is the direction Singer is suggesting, beyond our unthinking genetic impulses. Rational thought may then become a means for transcending our personal perspective by enabling us to universalize our thinking and so arrive at a wide, non-self-focused, all-embracing perspective. In this we return to our earlier dichotomy of self-involved and expansive. Our genes provide the ultimate blind and self-involved impulses, while rational thought provides us with a means for looking far beyond ourselves.

As we saw in Chapter Five, the view that rational thought offers us the means by which to move from a self-involved to expansive perspective reflects a developmental approach to morality. This also suggests that conscience, being centred on an internal process of thinking, similarly involves a developmental process.

MORAL DEVELOPMENT AND CONSCIENCE

Moral development, in the scale suggested by Ken Wilber, involves shifting from egocentric, to sociocentric, to worldcentric. But in order to achieve this shift in perspective, we first need to become aware of what in us is keeping us egocentric. This means becoming aware of the specific prejudices, social forces, family tendencies, or emotional attitudes, that keep us focused on ourselves.

In order to become aware, we need to examine how unconscious impulses and attitudes feed the gut feelings and inner voices that are associated with conscience. We would then be in a position to choose what to retain as useful to our developing moral perspective, and what to discard as not useful.

More specifically, such a process would require us to examine our assumptions regarding the moral codes that have come to us via our parents, peers, and the society in which we live, as well as the ideas that underpin each of the behaviors, rules, customs, and codes that exist in our society, whether they belong to the economic, social, legal, or religious spheres. This is necessary because before we can develop from self-involved decision-making to a wider perspective, we have to know where we are; before we can step forwards, we first have to know what holds us back. Conversely, there may be aspects of our life that are conducive to having a wider perspective. So we need to identify and retain what is useful to developing a universalizing moral perspective.

Thus for a developmental concept of conscience to work, we have to use rational thought to confront where we live, what we assume to be the case morally, and what we are psychologically, socially, and intellectually. The Fourth Way thinker, P.D. Ouspensky, defined conscience in this sense as "the state in which one cannot hide anything from oneself."[37]

Hence, as a working definition, conscience could be defined as the process of confronting and questioning the multi-leveled aspects of of the world, whether natural or human created, while also confronting our individual inner biological, psychological, intellectual, moral, and spiritual responses to that world.

This is far from a new thought. An attitude of self-examination or introspection has long been common in philosophic and religious traditions. Indeed, the phrase "examining our conscience" is frequently used in relation to the process of deciding what we think or how we will act when exercising moral choice.

> Some of the ancient philosophers—the Stoics in particular—studied to be blameless in their own sight, and for this they made frequent use of self-inspection. They professed the doctrine that the happiness and dignity of man consist in virtue, or compliance with the law of reason, or with conscience; and thus examinations of conscience were a regular practice in the schools of the Stoics and of their later followers, such Eclectics as Quintus Sextius and Seneca. In the hearts of all men there is heard at times the voice of conscience bidding them seek their moral perfection.[38]

This introduces a final concept in relation to conscience: that it is not only directed inwardly in a process of self-examination, it also requires us to look outwards from ourselves, towards a more moral process of decision-making. In the above quote this more moral process is called "moral perfection." It can be seen as the potential outcome of developing a greater moral sensibility.

What, then, does all this tell us about conscience? We can conclude that there is broad consensus regarding the following:

One: Conscience is not a "thing" existing within us. Rather, conscience is a process by which we exercise moral choice.

Two: Gut feelings or inner voices that tell us what is right or wrong are suspect at best, and at worst actually stop us exercising our moral choice (because they give us automatic, unthinking guidance on what to do).

Three: We need to use rational thought in order to exercise moral choice, because without rational thought we are not making a choice, we are mirroring what has been fed into us by biological and social impulses and forces.

Four: Exercising our conscience is a reflective activity which involves using rational thought to examine what we believe, think and do.

CONCLUSIONS REGARDING MORALITY

In these chapters I have examined the implications of both the morally subjective and morally objective perspectives, considering them in relation to our quest to find a moral yardstick that can be used in contemporary life. What, then, have we learned about being "good" in the modern world?

Clearly, morality exists on at least two levels: the collective social level, and the individual inward level. The collective social level has to do with how we treat others; it is the realm of ethics. Ethics concerns itself with our moral decision-making processes on a social level, in relation to our fellow humans beings. The individual inward level has to do with how we confront ourselves and our assumptions; it is the realm of conscience. From this point, conscience will be defined as concerning itself with our moral sensibility and self-awareness as it functions in relation to our inner attitudes and processes.

So ethics involves how we live with others, while conscience involves how we live with ourselves. From now on I will call morality as it functions on the outward social level ethics, and the inwardly-directed functioning of conscience I will term inner morality.

Rationality is important to both ethics and inner morality because without consciously deliberating on a moral choice we cannot make a choice. If we act without rationally thinking through the choices we have, then inevitably we are using gut feelings. And gut feelings tend to be narrow and self-involved, because they consist of inherited and conditioned beliefs, social customs, prejudices, and the like. So using rational thought is a key to developing ethically because it enables us to rise out of automatic, unthinking decision-making.

This movement is also linked to inward morality, which requires us to examine our own decision-making processes and to develop insight into how we and others make decisions. When we see limits in our decision-making process, particularly with respect to the moral beliefs, psychological responses, and ethical assumptions that prevent our perspective from shifting from self-involved to expansive, then we can remove those limiting factors. Only then do we have the opportunity to develop morally.

This suggests some interesting similarities between ethics and inner morality. However, before we make these connections there are more differences that need to be examined. For example, it has just been suggested that conscience is the key to inner morality. But how is this so? How specifically does conscience enable us to confront ourselves? What is the process? And what of virtues and vices? It has been suggested that virtues take us towards the good. In that case, what virtues apply in relation to inward morality? What vices? And what do virtues or vices contribute to our inner moral development?

Finally, there is the issue of the mystical perspective. Both wisdom and the mystical perspective lie at the heart of the moral and spiritual outlooks of Zarathushtra, the Buddha, and Plato. However, I haven't yet examined either in relation either to morality or to living a good life. Hence, in the next chapter I will move onto the examining all these in relation to the concept of inner morality and see what it can unfold to us about the moral yardstick we seek.

PART 5

ARE THERE LADDERS TO THE GOOD?

CHAPTER 11

What Good Is Conscience?

The previous chapter ended on a number of interesting questions in relation to inner morality. What is the role of conscience in relation to inner moral development? What does the practice of virtues contribute to inner moral development? What role does wisdom, especially mystic wisdom, have in relation to inner moral development? What kind of a developmental scale may plausibly be postulated in relation to inner morality?

I will examine the first three questions in this chapter, and the fourth in the next. Then I will look at the conclusions that can be drawn from what is found in relation to our quest for a moral yardstick. Let's begin with conscience.

In the previous chapter it was concluded that conscience with respect to inner morality may be characterized as a process of self-examination. Ouspensky defined conscience as "the state in which one cannot hide anything from oneself." I'll start this examination by reviewing what Zarathushtra, the Buddha, and Plato thought about conscience.

Those who follow the teachings of Zarathushtra call him *ahu*, an improving lord; *ratu*, a true guide; and *manthran*, a thought provoker. He named his teaching *Daênâ Vañuhi*, which is usually translated as the Good Religion, but which can also be interpreted to mean the Good Conscience.[1] For Zarathushtra, *daênâ* also exists within us as our conscience, which he defined as self-appraisal or self-perception. Zarathushtra considered that each person is a morally and spiritually autonomous being, that we each need to confront ourselves regarding what we believe and do, and that we have to take responsibility for the quality of our thoughts, words, and deeds as they manifest in our daily life. It is ourselves, not anyone else, who is responsible for what we think, say, and do. It is ourselves, not anyone else, who is responsible for our spiritual withering or growth. As Zarathushtra put it:

> Hear with your ears the best things. Reflect with clear purpose, each man for
> himself, on the two choices for decision.[2]

The two choices, of course, are the path of good and the path of evil. According to which we choose our inner self enters either the House of Good Purpose or the House of Worst Existence. However, for Zarathushtra our confrontation with evil not only occurs within us, but also in the world. Zarathushtra was an idealist, but he acknowledged that greedy, vicious people exist in the world, who in his day took others' cattle and land, and injured or killed to get what they wanted. Thus for Zarathushtra those who practice good conscience are not only obliged to think, say, and do good, but also to confront those who think, say, and do evil:

> Let those of good power rule with acts of understanding. Let not those of
> bad power rule over us ... Who will stop cruelty by bloodthirsty, wicked
> men? To whom will come the teaching of Good Purpose? They truly shall
> be saoshyants of the lands who follow knowledge of your teaching, Mazda,
> with Good Purpose, with acts inspired by truth. They indeed have been
> appointed opponents of Fury.[3]

Zarathustra himself was hounded by priests and the powerful of his day, to the extent that he was forced out of his own community. Yet he always advocated peaceful rather than violent confrontation. Thus while the Zoroastrian religion at its peak extended from the Middle East, across Central Asia, down into India, and over the border into China, conversion was done peacefully through discussion and example, not by force or sword.

Interestingly, the above passage introduces the concept of *saoshyant*, which literally means, "one who will bring benefit." Long after Zarathushtra, *saoshyant* came to be interpreted as a world savior, a spiritual being who would come some time in the future and save the world—an idea that lives on in Judaism's Messiah, Christianity's return of Jesus Christ, and Islam's Mahdi. Even Buddhism, long after the Buddha's time, developed the idea of a world savior called Maitreya.

However, as the above quotation also makes clear, Zarathushtra's idea was that each of us condemn or save ourselves according to our moral choices. Therefore, rather than there being a savior external to us, Zarathushtra called each person who utilized conscience and who followed the good path of asha, as being a *saoshyant* who brought benefit to themselves and others. Conscience for Zarathushtra thus provides us with a mechanism for confronting and, ultimately, changing not only ourselves, but also the culture in which we live.

One of the Buddha's great innovations was to position personal self-examination at the centre of his teaching. In the Buddha's view we are each wholly and completely responsible for our own spiritual salvation or demise:

> Do not be led by reports, or traditions, or hearsay. Do not be led by the authority of religious texts, nor by mere logic or inference, nor by considering appearances, nor by the delight in speculative opinions, nor by seeming possibilities, nor by the idea: "This is our teacher." But, O Kalamas, when you know for yourselves that certain things are unwholesome, wrong, and bad, then give them up … And when you know for yourselves that certain things are wholesome and good, then accept and follow them.[4]

The Buddha's teaching on self-examination and self-reliance went to the extreme of requiring his followers not to believe even what he told them, but to process all concepts, attitudes, and practices for themselves, whatever their source, and to decide, for themselves, what was right and wrong, useful or a hindrance. The Buddha was making the point that seekers too often follow others blindly, accept doctrines unthinkingly, and act without due rational process. He maintained that each of us should consider for ourselves any advice and guidance we receive—including his—before we decide how to apply and act on it.

Plato, for his part, did exactly this. He learned from his teacher, Socrates, that self-examination was the key to leading a philosophic life. That, as Socrates famously stated, "An unexamined life is not worth living." Socrates' view was that the practice of philosophy involved self-examination to discover the best way to live. As Socrates says in Plato's dialogue, *Gorgias*:

> What sort of person should one be? What should a person do with his life and how thoroughly should he devote himself to his chosen occupation? What should he be doing when he is young, and what should he be doing when he is older? The attempt to find the answer to these questions is the finest work in the world.[5]

Socrates' saw his work as a philosopher as consisting of questioning the assumptions Athenians made regarding how the good life should be lived, and what virtues, beliefs, and knowledge made the good life possible. In his pursuit of this task he very much applied Ouspensky's dictum of conscience as "the state in which one cannot hide anything from oneself." He questioned everyone who allowed him to, and showing them their false beliefs and wrong-headed thinking. Indeed, he succeeded so well in this work that eventually his fellow Athenians got sick of him and brought him to trial on the charges of denying the gods and of corrupting Athens' young. He was found guilty of both, and at the age of seventy-two was put to death by drinking hemlock.

Plato's early Socratic dialogues reflect the direction of Socrates' search for moral values. *Laches* enquires into the virtue of courage, *Lysis* investigates the nature of friendship, *Charmides* probes the virtue of self-control, and *Hippias Major* asks what makes something fine or elegant (as in a fine or elegant argument). In each of these dialogues Socrates challenged those he questioned, revealing that what they considered true knowledge to be nothing more than unconsidered opinions or self-contradictory ideas. Interestingly, in these early dialogues true knowledge is never achieved, with each discussion ending in a state of *aporia*, moral perplexity, and no definite conclusion being reached.

However, counterbalancing *aporia*, Socrates also saw himself as a philosophic midwife, helping those he questioned give birth to new concepts and approaches regarding how to live virtuously and happily. After Socrates' execution Plato explored what these new concepts and approaches to living might be, postulating that knowledge of the Good itself should be the philosopher's primary aim.

The Greek word *agathos*, which is usually translated into English as "good", has a greater range of meaning than good does in English. In English, good is primarily used in a passive sense, to refer to the excellent qualities a good person or good object possesses. However, in the original Greek, the primary meaning of *agathos* "always suggests to a Greek in the first place a reference of some kind to a purpose. One might almost say that the word means that which fulfils some purpose."[6] Hence, Socrates and Plato assumed not only that the good was something we naturally aspire towards, but also that because good was so obviously advantageous, no one would knowingly not seek it.

This was why living an examined life was so important—because by examining ourselves we gain knowledge of what is good that leads us to happiness, and of what is to be avoided because it takes us from the good and leads to unhappiness. In this Plato agrees with both Zarathushtra and the Buddha, that "when you know for yourselves that certain things are unwholesome, wrong, and bad, then give them up. ... And when you know for yourselves that certain things are wholesome and good, then accept them and follow them."

Conscience, then, as a process of questioning or enquiry, enables us to discern what these "certain things" are on two levels: within ourselves, and in the society in which we live.

CHAPTER 12

The Purpose Of Virtues And Wisdom

We have seen that the world's religious, philosophic, and spiritual traditions all advocate the practice of virtues. The English word virtue comes from the Latin, *virtus*, which was originally used in reference to the essence of manliness, that being valor.

In Medieval English the meaning of virtue widened to refer to the power or efficacy that anything possesses to achieve what it does, as in the 1623 statement, "If the Loadstone be of such virtue, let it show it by attracting the iron to it"[7]—i.e. the virtue of a magnet is that it possesses a magnetic field. By Victorian times the most common meaning of virtue had narrowed, being used to refer to moral virtues or, even more narrowly, to female chastity—an interesting journey for a word that began by describing the essence of manliness.

The Greek word *arête* corresponds to what we today call moral virtue. However, as with the Greek concept of *agathos* (good), for the Greeks *arête* had an active sense of "providing a quality which enables its possessor to do his work well or to attain his own end."[8]

Thus in terms of achieving a moral goal, virtues take us towards our goal and vices take us away from it. Virtues help us hit the mark; vices ensure we miss. The question then becomes, what is the mark or goal that we are aiming at?

THE VIRTUES FOR ZARATHUSHTRA

Zarathushtra saw humanity's goal as wisdom. What takes seekers towards wisdom is the path of asha. And it is through the practice of the Zoroastrian virtues that one walked the path.

The virtues were nowhere definitively listed by Zarathushtra. However, in his *Gathas,* Zarathushtra consistently referred to six virtuous qualities. These are: *vohu manah* (good mind, good thinking), which manifests in discerning thought; *asha* (truth, order, righteousness), which requires practitioners to recognize transcendent spiritual reality and manifests pragmatically in doing "the right thing, at the right time, and with the right means in order to attain the right result"; *khshathra* (power, dominion), which manifests as benevolent rule in the world, but also refers to acknowledging the divine in all actions; *âramaiti* (tranquillity, stability), which manifests socially as peace and religiously as holiness and devotion; *seraosha* (listening within); and *daênâ* (conscience).[9]

The wisdom these virtues led to was characterized as consisting of *haurvatât* (wholeness, completion) and *ameretât* (immortality). These two qualities were the spiritual goal of Zarathushtra's teaching.

THE VIRTUES FOR BUDDHA

Numerous virtues are enumerated in Buddhism. However, the essence of the Buddha's teaching on the virtues is contained in the Eightfold Noble Path, which lists eight virtues as the key to Buddhist practice: right speech, right action, right livelihood, right effort, right mindfulness, right concentration, right thought, and right understanding.

These eight virtues are divided into three levels: *sila,* pertaining to ethical conduct; *samadhi,* pertaining to mental discipline and self-mastery; and *prajna,* pertaining to wisdom.

The three virtues that function on the level of ethical conduct are right speech, right action, and right livelihood.[10] Right speech involves not telling lies; not speaking in ways that promote enmity, hatred and dissension; not using malicious or abusive language; and not engaging in idle babble. Right action involves promoting moral, honourable, and peaceful conduct, and not engaging in stealing, dishonesty, illegitimate sex, or destructive acts. Right livelihood involves not having an occupation that brings harm or hurt to others. Clearly, these three core virtues pertain to ethical conduct in the sphere of social interaction.

The next level of virtues consists of right effort, right mindfulness, and right concentration, which together pertain to the inner practices of mental discipline and self-mastery. Right effort involves actively working to eradicate unwholesome and evil thoughts, attitudes, and states, and to promoting positive and nurturing thoughts, attitudes, and states. Right mindfulness involves giving attention to, and being watchful of, the body's activities, emotional states, the mind's movements, and what is occurring in the external world. Right concentration involves meditation and maintaining silent, focused, one-pointed concentration. Together, these three virtues lead the practitioner within, providing a pathway towards knowledge and the experience of transcendental reality.

The third level, *prajna* or wisdom, consists of the virtues of right thought and right understanding. Right thought involves promoting "thoughts of selfless renunciation or detachment, thoughts of love, and thoughts of non-violence, which are extended to all beings."[11] It results from the change in thinking that is accomplished at the second level of self-mastery. Right understanding involves understanding how the world is, and how we experience our existence in it.

For the Buddha, self-discipline and self-mastery were the keys to achieving the ultimate goal of experiencing the mystic state of nirvana. Nonetheless, he never forgot that a mystic lives in the world with others, teaching that moral and ethical conduct laid the foundation for mystical experience, and that we need to live well with others in order to live well inside ourselves. Love, gentleness, kindness, and respect were additional virtues that help us achieve this goal. For the Buddha, compassion and wisdom were two keys to living the good life. Compassion provided the key to social interaction with others, and wisdom the key to living with our selves.

THE VIRTUES FOR PLATO

Plato considered the goal of human existence was to live a good and happy life, and that the good life is achieved through practicing the four virtues of wisdom, courage, moderation, and justice.

Wisdom was significant because it was both a virtue in itself, and the goal towards which the good life led. Wisdom "is what is common to all the virtues. One who possesses this virtue [wisdom] will possess them all, for anyone who is wise will recognise what he or she should do in all morally relevant circumstances and contexts."[12] Thus we cannot be just without being wise as to what justice is, or moderate without being wise as to what moderation is, or courageous without being wise as to what courage is.

In his later dialogues, Plato expanded on Socrates' ideas by relating the four virtues to the three parts of the soul. These are: the rational part, which manifests via our intellect when we engage in rational thought; the spirited part, which manifests via our will when we engage in the struggles of everyday life; and the appetitive part, which manifests in the body's wants and desires. Plato considered that the virtue of wisdom belongs to the rational part of the soul, which should rule the soul's other parts. The virtue of courage involves facing a situation knowingly, being aware of the consequences, but still doing what has to be done. The virtue of moderation belongs to our appetitive soul, which always needs to be kept in check by moderation.

Plato argued that the virtue of justice involves harmony and balance. Justice on the social level requires us to bring the variously discordant parts of society into harmonious balance, while justice on the individual level involves harmonizing the rational, spirited, and appetitive parts of the soul. In this way the four virtues of wisdom, courage, moderation, and justice enable both a society as a whole, and individuals within that society, to live not just the good life, but also a wise life.

However, for Plato, wisdom didn't just involve moral knowledge. Wisdom also had a metaphysical aspect. This meant that the ultimate goal of the philos-

---

THREE APPROACHES TO THE VIRTUES

ZARATHUSHTRA

Six virtuous qualities:
- Good thinking
- Truth, order, right
- Power, dominion
- Tranquility, stability
- Listening within
- Conscience

These virtues lead to the acquisition of:
- Wholeness, completion
- Immortality

BUDDHA

Eight virtues:
- Right speech
- Right action
- Right livelihood
- Right effort
- Right mindfulness
- Right concentration
- Right thought
- Right understanding

These virtues lead to:
- Wisdom
- Nirvana

PLATO

Four virtues:
- Wisdom
- Courage
- Moderation
- Justice

Practiced in relation to:
- Rational soul
- Spirited soul
- Appetitive soul

These vitues enable:
- Ascent from sensible realm to intelligible realm to mystic realm

FIGURE 12.1

opher's efforts was achieving knowledge of the Good directly, through mystic perception. Further, just as the Buddha taught that there were three phases in his Eightfold Noble Path, so Plato considered there were three stages to attaining mystic wisdom. He defined these three stages as sensible, intelligible, and mystical.

The sensible stage is our everyday life, experience via the senses. Plato considered human existence on this level is characterized by a disharmony of virtues and a predominance of vices. Ruled by the appetites, our energy uncontrolled, and everything in us out of balance, our thought is led astray by illusory ideas and misleading opinions. Thus, individually and as a society, we lack true knowledge. This lack manifests in the way we become caught up in appearances, mistake pleasure for happiness, chase desires that can never be satisfied, are led astray by political rhetoric, and too often perceive injustice as justice.

But if we engage in the philosophic life, and if we practice the moral virtues of courage, justice, moderation, and wisdom, we progressively purify our soul, limiting vices and progressively bringing our soul's three parts into harmony with each other. In the resultant state of inner harmony, the philosopher is then able to ascend internally from the sensible realm into the intelligible realm, where he or she starts to gather knowledge of moral goods such as justice, courage, and moderation; mathematical goods such as geometry and music; and philosophic goods such as beauty and truth.

In his explanation of the ascent into the intelligible realm, Plato likened the philosopher's soul to a chariot that is flown across the sky by two winged horses, one white, one black. The white horse is good, modest, moderate, and obedient, and is naturally inclined towards the heavens, while the black horse is unruly, insolent, proud, and wicked, and is inclined to fly down towards the earth. Black and white, good and bad, obedient, and unruly—we are back at Zarathushtra's distinction between the divergent paths that lead either to life or to non-life.

In order to sustain the ascent into the intelligible realm, the philosopher is tasked with purifying his or her soul by using the moral virtues. These enable the philosopher to bring the black horse under control. If sufficient moral control is achieved, the white horse leads the soul up into the divine; if not, the soul loses its wings and the black horse plunges it down to the earth and back into the ignorance and disharmony of sensual existence.

The realm of the intelligible is attained through self-control, purification, and intellectual apprehension. However, philosophers who continue to purify and harmonize their soul fly up even higher, into the mystic realm, where the philosopher's goal is achieved: perception of the Good. Plato identified the Good with God. Both were perceived through mystic perception:

> The elimination of evil is impossible, Theodorus: there must always be some force ranged against good. But it is equally impossible for evil to be stationed in heaven; its territory is necessarily mortal nature—it patrols this earthly realm. That is why one should try to escape as quickly as possible from here to there. The escape-route is assimilation to God, in so far as this is possible, and this assimilation is the combination of wisdom with moral respect for God and man. ... It is utterly and completely impossible for God to be immoral and not to be the acme of morality; and the only way any of us, for our part, can approximate to God is to become as moral as possible. ... To recognize this is true wisdom and virtue; not to recognize it is proof of ignorance and evil.[13]

The philosopher's ascent from the sensible earthly realm to direct experience of God in the mystic realm results from "the combination of wisdom with moral respect for God and man."

Thus, in agreement with Zarathushtra and the Buddha, Plato saw the good, morality, and wisdom as being the means of ascent towards transcendental spiritual reality, a reality that may equally be called Ahura Mazda, nirvana, or the Good.

CHAPTER 13

Ascending To The Mystic Good

Zoroastrianism, Buddhism, and Platonic philosophy each consider that virtues associated with both external ethical behavior and inner morality provide the foundation for living the good life. Each tradition makes clear that when seekers practice ethical and inner virtues, that practice enables them to ascend to wisdom. And wisdom involves a direct mystic apprehension of transcendent reality.

But these three traditions are not alone in maintaining this perspective. For example, India's yogic practices postulate two levels of moral practice, *yama* and *niyama*. *Yama* is outwardly-directed and ethical in scope, and comprises five aspects: not stealing, not killing, truthfulness, self-restraint, and not receiving gifts (that is, being independent). *Niyama* is inwardly-directed and similarly has five aspects: practicing cleanliness, contentment, austerity, study, and surrendering the sense of self.[14]

As Swami Vivekananda observed: "The *Yama* and *Niyama*, as we see, are moral trainings; without these as the basis no practice of yoga will succeed. As these become established, the yogi will begin to realize the fruits of his practice; without these it will never bear fruit."[15] The ultimate aim of yogic practice is to achieve the mystic state of samadhi, which is sustained inner concentration.

A second example is offered by Judaism, which teaches the concept of *tikkun*, mending or perfecting. This concept manifests outwardly in the long-standing tradition of *tikkun olam*, which involves the mending of the world through helping society develop morally, and especially through working to establish social justice. But there is also inward, mystic tikkun. In the sixteenth century classic, *Shaarey Kedushah* (*Gates of Holiness*), Rabbi Chaim Vital described both the theory and practice of Kabbalistic meditation. This includes a practice that he traced back to the prophet Elijah. Rabbi Vital quoted Elijah as saying:

> I call heaven and earth to witness that any individual, man or woman, Jew
> or gentile, freeman or slave, can have Ruach HaKodesh [the Holy Spirit,
> by which the transcendent is experienced] come upon him. It all depends
> on his deeds.[16]

The deeds Rabbi Vital identified included moral purification, which began with the repentance of every sin the practitioner has done, and rectifying the resulting pain and damage. Purification also involved keeping the positive Commandments, developing concentration through prayer, studying sacred texts, adopting the physical disciplines of eating and sleeping sparely, maintaining bodily purity, developing psychological purity by eliminating unworthy character traits, becoming solitary, and not speaking unnecessarily.[17]

As another sixteenth century rabbi, Moshe Cordevero, observed: "When a person is upright and righteous, he can meditate with appropriate thoughts, and ascend through the levels of the transcendental."[18] Thus it is only after a practitioner has sufficiently purified his or her inner state that meditation will be successful.

From these two examples, and from the concepts explored in the previous chapter, we see that the moral purification achieved through the practice of virtues has two uses. The first is it helps us become better people, in relation to our fellow citizens. The second is it helps us become more spiritually knowing, in an inward sense of experiencing and understanding our inner selves and our spiritual nature. Each use involves a process of moral development.

I considered Kohlberg's model of ethical development in Chapter Nine. It would be helpful to identify a similar model in relation to inner morality.

A MODEL FOR THE INNER MORALITY

This model needs to reflect the moral development that, to use the terms of Platonic philosophy, provides seekers with a basis for ascending from the sensual-sensible, through the conceptual-intelligible, to the mystic realm. Because mystic experience is the ultimate goal of inner morality, it would also be useful to construct a developmental model that leads to transcendent spiritual experience.

Interestingly, we have already considered the inverse of this process in Chapter Nine, when I suggested how religions originate in their founder's spiritual experiences, then progressively descend through seven steps. They eventually end up as rigid lists and dogmatic religious formulae. The development of inner morality involves the opposite of this descent. It consists of an ascent from ignorance and non-apprehension to an inner state of transcendent mystical insight. Accordingly, the following model (see FIGURE 13.1) uses the descending stages that have previously been identified, but inverts them to create a template for identifying the stages of inner moral development.

Step One. Anyone who wishes to develop morally starts from a state of moral immaturity, focused on personal situations, wants and needs, ignorant of, or not caring about, the wider implications and impact of their decision-making. Plato used traditional religious language to identify ignorant decision-making with vice and sin. Alternatively, making use of contemporary secular terminology, we could say that at this lowest level self-interest is paramount and concern with the detrimental consequences of our actions on others is at best minimal, at worst non-existent. Or we could use the metaphysical language of the mysteries and say that such people live in the outer darkness. Those living actively on this moral level initiate actions that oppress, exploit, or harm others. However, the majority of people live passively on this level, unthinkingly accepting the actions of those who oppress, exploit, or harm others, and are frequently oppressed, exploited, or hurt ourselves.

Step two. This requires waking up, which in turn means seeing what is going on in the world around us, and beginning to inwardly perceive our own personal moral weaknesses. Reading across the above model, we can see that the seventh step on the descending octave relates to institutionalization and rules, while the second step of the ascending octave involves waking up to the impact institutions have on our world and the way they end up dominating our existence. Many people live at this second step, fighting multinational, national, customary, communal, or familial institutional power, whether through confrontation or by striving to extract themselves from it.

Socrates saw his principle role as being to wake Athenians up to their psychological and moral situation on this level. In questioning his fellow citizens, he sought to wake them up to their unexamined assumptions and self-justifications. Today we have environmentalists, health professionals, journalists, lobbyists, psychologists, scientists, religionists, intellectuals, and sociologists all similarly trying to wake us up to truths about our shared existence that they consider significant.

The key to waking up is adopting a new perspective on whatever we're looking at—whether that be with respect to the environment, the economy, our occupation, our behavior, our attitudes, our responsibilities, our psychological make-up, our dissatisfactions, our weaknesses, our possibilities, our unhappiness, or our soul. In religious terms, this step involves a conversion experience. The Greeks called such an experience *metanoia*, which means transformation of mind, transformation of thought. Literally, *metanoia* can be interpreted as "turning our thought around."[19] Waking up and seeing things in a new way is the start of any new development, moral or otherwise.

Step three. This step involves transforming the second step of waking up and seeing things from a new perspective into sustained struggle. Self-questioning and practicing virtues enable us to do this. Self-questioning helps us extend our new perspective, through the activities of thinking, researching, and seeking advice from others. Practicing virtues helps us fight against the assumptions, attitudes, and habits that have for so long sustained our ignorant, self-involved viewpoint. People often join groups of like-minded people at this third step in order to sustain the momentum they have developed and to obtain advice

THE DESCENT OF SPIRITUAL EXPERIENCE TO RELIGION				THE ASCENT FROM IGNORANCE TO SPIRITUAL EXPERIENCE
Transcendent experience	1	8		Transcendent experience
Non-verbal guidance	2	7		Inwardness
Verbal teaching	3	8		Deepened experience
First deflection				Second shock: Internal
Creation of texts	4	5		Transformation of being
Codification	5	4		Accessing higher knowledge
Second deflection				First shock: External
Literalization, dogma	6	3		Struggle, questioning, virtues
Institutionalization, rules	7	2		Waking up, new perspectives
Suppression	8	1		Self-involvement, ignorance

FIGURE 13.1

regarding what they need to do next. For some people this step involves joining a religious or spiritual group to help them in their struggle; for others it involves leaving their religion, group, or life situation—if it is controlling, oppressing, or damaging them—and seeking a more nurturing environment.

External shock. After the third step a natural pause occurs. This is because, having reached the third level of development, many find such an inner state is sufficient. They have opened themselves up, developed some of their possibilities, and are no longer in the ignorant, unhappy, dissatisfied, or self-involved states that previously dominated their lives. Possibly they have overcome the habits that were damaging them, established a positive balance in their daily existence, or have joined a community that makes them feel accepted, comfortable, and nurtured. Yet step four still waits, offering the next developmental step. Obviously, if a seeker remains at level three this knowledge cannot be accessed. So this pause has to be jumped over. What enables us to make the jump from the third to the fourth step is a shock. Usually this shock is provided by an experience that temporarily forces us out of the comfort zone that is level three and that makes us realize there is much greater knowledge yet to be achieved.

Ramana Maharshi, the twentieth century Indian mystic, experienced such a shock at the age of seventeen, when he suddenly felt strange, lay down on the floor, and rapidly became convinced he was going to die. This feeling then mutated into a mystic experience so powerful that, after he had recovered, he left his home and started on the path of meditation that he practiced for the rest of his life.[20] Paul of Tarsus experienced a similar shock when, on the road to Damascus, he heard what he thought was the voice of God. This so transformed him that he joined the spiritual groups he had previously been prosecuting. For others, this type of shock may occur as the result of a life-threatening accident, through the impact of life events, or from meeting a person whose words, presence, or actions cause them to question the principles by which they live. What distinguishes this shock from the metanoia experience of step two is that the metanoia experience shows us how things *are* inside or outside us, while the "road to Damascus" shock shows us how things *could be* within.

As a result of this experiential shock, the seeker now ascends to step four. The equivalent step on the descending octave is the codification of the founder's teaching. The higher knowledge revealed by step four on the ascending octave results from our starting to see through the surface words of this codification and into what the religious founders' codified teachings signify spiritually. This insight is possible because the practitioner has had a transformative "Damascus" experience. While this experience is at a much lower level than that experienced by spiritual geniuses such as the Buddha, Moses, Jesus, or Muhammad, nonetheless the knowledge experienced at this step provides a key by which the higher teachings within religions and sacred texts may begin to be unlocked.

Step five. This step involves using this newly-acquired knowledge to continue inner development. Such knowledge becomes consolidated internally through the continued practice of virtues. An example of the required virtues is provided by the three virtues of mental discipline and self-mastery from the Buddha's Eightfold Noble Path—right effort, right mindfulness, and right concentration. Step five is also a creative level. The equivalent step in the descending octave involves encapsulating the founders' teachings in metaphorical and symbolic ritual, art and texts. Step five of the ascending octave involves developing an intuitive, creative response to those texts and artworks. Some seekers who possess an artistic talent are also able to create such ritual, art, or texts themselves. It could be argued that this is what religions today need to keep them spiritually relevant; not priests and religious authorities who endlessly repeat words from the distant past, but the insights and spiritual momentum of contemporary practitioners who experience higher levels of knowledge as a result of practicing inner virtues.

Internal shock. A second pause exists between steps five and six. This pause occurs because step five is another level at which a seeker may comfortably remain. In order to continue ascending, the seeker is challenged continuously to give up what has been achieved in order to enter what has not yet been achieved. The shock of a "Damascus experience" comes from outside us and transforms our experience of life, opening us up to the reality of higher levels. This second shock involves an enlightenment experience that occurs as a result of our efforts at self-transformation, and that centres us even more firmly in our spiritual self. Different traditions have various names to refer to this experience. For Zen Buddhists it involves a break-through or enlightenment experience. In Sufism it is referred to as dying before you die. In Vedanta it is the stage of escaping the rounds of births and deaths. In mystical Christianity this shock is referred to as a spiritual death followed by the virgin birth, a process that is also called the birth of the resurrection body. The Jewish mystics and Gnostics considered that at this stage the practitioner receives a robe of glory.

Step six. Previously the seeker drew wisdom from sacred texts, from the guidance of others, and from personal experience. At step six the seeker has access to wisdom in a much higher, intense, and direct form. Looking across on the graphic, the equivalent step on the descending octave is verbal teaching. The seeker at the sixth step of the ascending octave now finds he or she is able to speak directly from personal experience. In addition, because by this time years have been spent on the ascending path, the seeker has undergone many experiences, thought through many aspects of the path he or she is on, and has seen what others have succeeded at or have failed to achieve. All this knowledge and experience provides further material from which to speak. Of course, anyone can speak from personal experience at any step of the ascending octave. What differentiates this step from the others below it is that the seeker is able to speak with certainty and authority on religious and spiritual matters at a high level. The effort required to reach this step has provided him or her with numerous intuitive insights, given clarity of purpose, and provided a depth of understanding that is not available to the rest of us. At this step the seeker is putting together the spiritual path in a profoundly mystical way.

Steps seven and eight. The next two steps, inwardness and transcendent experience, deepen this mystical experience even further. Inwardness consists of maintaining a connection with the spiritual self. Transcendent experience involves an experience even higher than that experienced between steps five and six. This eighth step is the Platonic mystic philosopher's experience of the Good, in which he or she is assimilated to God. It is also Zarathushtra's experience of Ahura Mazda. Indian mystical Vedanta differentiates between two states of samadhi (a concentrated state achieved through meditation or silent prayer). These are samadhi with seed, that is, experience of transcendent reality with a sense of self attached, and samadhi without seed, experience of transcendent reality with no sense of self. Samadhi without seed is what the Buddha experienced under the bodhi tree. He called this experience nirvana. The transcendent experience at step eight involves transcending not just the sensible and intelligible spheres, but also the self that experiences those spheres. At this step the seeker loses his or her sense of self and gains a profound spiritual knowledge—both of which are at the opposite end of the scale from the self-involvement and ignorance that dominate those living at step one.

It can be seen that the three phases of this ascending octave correspond to Plato's and the Buddha's developmental scales. Thus steps 1, 2, and 3 reflect

Plato's sensible realm and the Buddha's category of ethical conduct; steps 4 and 5 reflect Plato's intelligible realm and the Buddha's category of mental disciple and self-mastery; and steps 6, 7, and 8 reflect Plato's mystic sphere and the Buddha's category of wisdom.

A LADDER OF INNER VIRTUES

One further point needs to be made before finishing this part of the discussion. It is that while the seeker's moral ascent has been divided into eight steps, which the model suggests are made progressively, one after another, in practice it often doesn't work out so straightforwardly.

Arguably, the experience of dying that Ramana Maharshi underwent took him straight from step one to steps four and five. Clearly, the Maharshi was an exceptional case, although Indian seekers would say he jumped so far in one leap because of the effort he had made in previous lives.

More usual is regularly jumping back and forth between steps, or occupying more than one step simultaneously. For example, anyone at steps two or three could engage in the practice of inwardness. Because their inner being is not developed, and because they do not have access to the understanding available to those at step six, such seekers will not experience inwardness at the intensity that those at step seven do. Nonetheless, an experience of inwardness may be achieved at any lower level. Similarly another seeker may have a high-level experience early in their search, but then require years to assimilate its implications and to bed it down within. Thus this model should be seen as a template to aid our understanding of a complex process, and not interpreted as a dogmatic attempt to fix all things into one single definitive scale.

In conclusion, it is now clear that inner morality is significant because it provides the foundations for spiritual development. In particular, externally-directed ethical virtues on the one hand, and internally-directed inner morality virtues on the other, provide the two legs on which stands the ladder that we ascend in our quest for mystic experience. Without these two legs of outer and inner there can be no ladder, and therefore no ascent.

PART 6

LIVING THE GOOD LIFE

CHAPTER 14

How Good Is It To Be Human?

We are approaching the end of our quest. I began by asking what a moral yardstick that we could use in the modern world might look like. It is now time to summarize what has been discovered. First, I identified two broad areas of morality: ethics and inner morality.

Ethics is externally-directed and functions in relation to our collective social interaction, while inner morality is internally-directed and functions in relation to our personal spiritual growth. Five aspects are fundamental when considering the values each adds to our lives. These are: context, goal, means, virtues, and a developmental scale. I will briefly review first ethics, then inner morality, to see what each contributes to a moral yardstick.

WHAT IS THE GOOD FOR ETHICS?

Ethical context. I'll start by reviewing what we have learned with respect to ethics by considering the context within which we think and live. We have seen how European thinkers who lived between the seventeenth and nineteenth centuries developed the political, economic, and social concepts that subsequently shaped contemporary Western societies. In particular, we saw how Immanuel Kant, Adam Smith, Jeremy Bentham, and J.S. Mill advocated a range of significant concepts. These included the idea that morality should come from within rather than from divine decree, and that Western societies should separate the powers of the church and the state—an idea that laid the social and political foundations for today's secular societies. Allied to this separation were the ideas that the ideal political system for a secular state is democracy; that the ideal economic system is the free market; that right and wrong should ultimately be decided in our courts, according to legal process; and that each citizen should have inalienable freedoms and rights, which are epitomized in liberal religious, economic, and personal freedoms, including the right to education, work, and to vote, and freedom of movement, assembly, and speech.

In the process of transforming societies into secular liberal democracies, the previous religiously-derived moral objectivist ethics that had held sway in European countries for hundred of years was jettisoned and replaced by moral relativism. This is the idea that morality is essentially a social construct, which from a wider perspective results from cultural norms, and from a narrower perspective results from individual choice. But in either case there is no single objective standard by which moral judgments validly may be made. At the extreme end of this moral perspective is the view that any society, or any individual, may do whatever the wish, as long as it accords either with social norms, or with individual choice. Thus on the social level, if a society's norms dictate that female babies are a burden on a family and therefore should be killed at birth, then it is moral to kill them' and on the social level, if an individual decides taking what others have is the right way to live, then that is acceptable ethical behavior.

However, in practice most people consider that neither societies, nor individuals in a society, should be able to do whatever they want, and that there should be limits placed on our behavior. Ideas regarding what these limits might be, and how they would function to curb those who harm others' freedoms and rights, were developed over several centuries—indeed, are still developing today. Initially, Kant suggested the idea of duty as an ethical curb, while Adam Smith offered natural sympathy as a limit to naked self-interest. Neither idea was widely accepted. However, in the nineteenth century J. S. Mill suggested that people should be able to do as they wish, but only as long as they did not harm others. This idea became formalized his "harm principle." Mill's ethical concept struck a chord, and his harm principle has become a moral principle most Westerners agree with today. Other curbs that lead to socially acceptable behavior are provided by long-established social norms, traditional customary practices and, of course, society's laws. This means that, in practice, Western nations function ethically according to a softened form of moral relativism, by which citizens have the right to do what they wish, as long as they act within socially defined limits.

Ethical goals. Having clarified the context, the next question becomes: What should be a society's ethical goal? In a religious society the goal is clearly serving God and his absolute Word. In a secular, morally relativist society, the society itself has to decide what its shared ethical goal should be. Mill, taking his lead from the Greeks, suggested individual happiness should be the goal. This idea is reflected in the United States Bill of Rights, which asserts that all citizens have a right to the pursuit of happiness. Alternatively, the French constitution defines the highest social goal as fraternity, equality, and liberty. Other thinkers have suggested social justice, the free market, globalization, equal opportunity, democracy, care for the environmental, individual accumulation of wealth, and universal care as ultimate social goods and goals.

The point of a society having an ultimate social goal is that it provides that society with its highest concept of social good by which it may measure its approach towards, or movement away from, the good. Clearly, while Western cultures collectively have not agreed on any single ultimate social good, the smaller goods of personal happiness, individual freedoms, sexual and racial equality, the right to accumulate wealth, and various forms of social care, together constitute a broad Western concept of ultimate social good.

With respect to defining social goals on an individual level, utilitarian ethical philosopher Peter Singer suggests that we should use rational thought to universalize our ethical goals. Rational thought also provides a means for deciding what and how social goals should be achieved. For Singer this process requires individual citizens to put aside their personal wants and desires, and instead attempt to view ethical issues from the perspective of all those who will be affected by the decision. That way those involved will collectively decide on a course of action that will satisfy as many of those affected as possible.

Finally, having considered all these, and having recognized what was common to them all, it was suggested that our ultimate social good should be nurturing our individual and collective human potential. This means that the moral value of decisions and actions should be assessed on the basis of whether they diminish or enhance our collective and individual humanity.

Accordingly, decisions and actions that oppress, degrade, or harm an individual should be deemed to be unethical and bad, while decisions and actions that respect, nurture, and enhance an individual's human potential should be considered ethical and good.

Ethical means. Having established an ultimate social good, the next question is how should a society achieve that good? What means should be adopted in order to achieve it? For example, many business people and economists consider that the accumulation of individual wealth should be the highest social good, and that the free market coupled to minimal government intervention offer the best means for achieving that goal. Self-interest is considered to provide the principle by which the free market most effectively functions. On the other hand, for those who consider preserving Western secular, culturally pluralist democracies to be a society's greatest good, the package of freedoms and rights that contribute to the democratic process provides the means by which that may be achieved.

Finally, if the highest social goal is considered to be the enhancement of citizens' collective and individual humanity, then the best means for evaluating whether an action takes us towards that goal is rational thought. Social norms, customary practices, communal rules, and national and international laws each have to be considered rationally. If any of these diminish citizens' human potential through being oppressive, exploitative or harmful, then they need to be changed.

Ethical virtues. Practicing virtues also enables a society to achieve its chosen social goals. We saw that in order for secular, culturally pluralist, democratic Western societies to achieve their moral goals, citizens have to practice certain liberal and social virtues. This is because today the citizens of Western societies come from divergent cultural, religious, racial, language, and social backgrounds. Blending different peoples into a single society requires each citizen putting aside limiting and narrow attitudes such as fear, intolerance, resentment, and self-interest, and replace them with virtues such as respecting others' ways of eating, dressing, talking, and living. It also requires practicing virtues such as acceptance, tolerance, understanding, and mutual respect, with rational thought used to work through differences.

Ethical development. To achieve all this citizens need to grow from intolerant to tolerant, from fearful to understanding, and from judgmental to accepting. This gives rise to the question of a model of ethical development. Whether we adopt Kohlberg's model, or prefer the alternative stages suggested by Gilligan or Wilber, ethical development ultimately involves taking a universal rather than self-interested view. As Peter Singer observes:

> An ethical principle cannot be defended in relation to any partial or sectional view. Ethics takes a universal point of view. ... In making ethical judgments we go beyond our own likes and dislikes. From an ethical point of view, the

fact that it is I who benefits from, say, a more equal distribution of income and you who lose by it, is irrelevant. Ethics requires us to go beyond 'I' and 'you' to the universal law, the universalizerable judgment, the standpoint of the impartial spectator or ideal observer. [1]

Thus for pluralist, liberal democracies to function to their moral potential, citizens have to put aside their personal interests, develop a universalized perspective, and embrace ethical decisions that benefit the greatest number of citizens as possible.

WHAT IS THE GOOD FOR INNER MORALITY?

Moral context. The context for inner morality is internal. It functions with respect to our psycho-spiritual awareness. This awareness demarcates the world in which we live into three levels: the everyday sensible level that we experience through our senses; the intelligible level that we access via rational thought; and the mystical level that we experience spiritually.

Moral goal. The goal of inner morality is for us to develop our awareness so that we are able to apprehend each of these three levels of the world. At the pinnacle of this awareness is what Zarathushtra called Ahura Mazda, Wisdom. In practice, we accumulate wisdom during our perceptual journey upwards, through the three levels of reality, culminating in mystical apprehension of transcendent reality.

Moral means. The means by which we journey upwards is conscience and virtues. Conscience is, in Ouspensky's words, "the state in which one cannot hide anything from oneself." It consists of a process of self-examination, in which we question all the assumptions we make regarding the customs, beliefs, and rules into which we are born. We also have to examine our psychological make-up, the economic, social, political, intellectual, metaphysical, and religious concepts that have shaped us, the ethical choices we make, and the way we act when enacting our choices. Using conscience enables us to critique all these assumptions and actions, to take them apart to see how they are constituted, then to put them back together into a new psychological, moral, and spiritual whole, keeping those concepts that are useful and discarding the rest.

Conscience in this sense can be applied to the society in which we live as much as to each of us as individuals. The criteria that was postulated in relation to ethics, of deciding whether we are doing good or bad according to whether we are enhancing or harming our shared humanity, can also apply to inner morality. Conscience, then, involves the use of rational thought to question the assumptions on which our society functions and to challenge those whose actions limit or harm the potential of other beings.

At the heart of this confrontation is a recognition that we have a fundamental choice in our lives. We can go either the way of the good, or the way of the bad. Hence individually or collectively we can enter, in Zarathushtra's words, the House of Best Purpose, or the House of Worst Existence. As a result of the choices we make we enter one of these two "houses"—which are really just social and inner states of being that we create for ourselves through the choices we make.

VIRTUES FOR ETHICS AND INNER MORALITY

ETHICAL VIRTUES	INNER MORALITY VIRTUES
• Context: Ethical virtues are created and applied within a specific social community.	• Context: Inner morality virtues are created and applied within the individual.
• Goal: That community needs to agree on ultimate social goals.	• Goal: The acquisition of wisdom on sensible, intelligible and mystic levels.
• Means: The community then needs to use rational thought to decide on the best means for achieving that goal without oppressing, exploiting or harming others.	• Means: Utilizing conscience as self-examination which is achieved through rational thought, and identifying and choices the path which leads to the realization of the goal
• Virtues: The community adopts qualities and attitudes conducive to achieving ultimate social goals.	• Virtues: The sensible virtues of social ethics, the intelligible virtues of self-mastery, the mystic wisdom virtues
• Development: Each member of the community shifts from a self-interested and involved perspective to a universalized perspective that achieves the agreed ultimate goals for the greatest number.	• Development: Eight stages of mystic ascent: starting in ignorance; waking up; struggling; accessing higher knowledge; transforming self; deepening experience; developing inwardness; experiencing transcendence.

FIGURE 14.1

Moral virtues. Virtues and vices provide us with the attitudes and practices by which we act and behave. We saw that the Buddha divided the virtues into three categories: the ethical virtues, the self-mastery virtues, and the wisdom virtues. The ethical virtues are the same as those virtues that apply to social ethics. However, where social ethics look outwards, inner morality highlights the inner aspect of those virtues. The self-mastery virtues include concentration, balance, and mindfulness. These are virtues that help us develop our inner potential and ascend within ourselves to higher levels of understanding. The wisdom virtues consist of right thought and right understanding. Right thought echoes Singer's idea of universalized ethical thought, but it offers the inner aspect of this idea by emphasizing an individual practice of selflessness and of love which is extended to all beings.

Moral development. Practicing the inner virtues helps us ascend within ourselves to higher levels of being, knowledge, and understanding. This assumes there is a scale of development by which we may ascend from a state of ignorance to one of wisdom. I have proposed a developmental model that identified the eight key steps in this ascent as: 1. Self-involvement and ignorance; 2. Waking up to a new perspective; 3. Struggling, questioning and practicing virtues; 4. Accessing higher knowledge; 5. Transforming being; 6. Deepening experience; 7. Developing spiritual inwardness; and 8. Experiencing transcendence.

Obviously, various religious and spiritual traditions have their own stages and models for describing inner development which reflect their specific concepts and practices. The purpose of the proposed model was to provide a set of generalized terms that could be useful in relation to any religion or tradition.

But whatever model is used, and however we may define the various virtues of inner morality, their significance lie in the way they lay a foundation for spiritual development:

> The Yama and Niyama, as we see, are moral trainings; without these as the basis no practice of yoga will succeed. As these become established, the yogi will begin to realize the fruits of his practice.[2]

These words of Vivekananda equally apply to all religious and spiritual traditions. Without the two legs of ethics and inner morality, the ladder of spiritual ascent cannot be climbed.

CHAPTER 15

Defining The Moral Yardstick

Having examined these two spheres of moral activity, it is now time to assemble what we have learned about ethics and ethical development, and inner morality and its development, and draw some conclusions regarding what a contemporary Western moral yardstick could look like.

First, previous considerations have made it clear that we are not dealing with an old-fashioned, one-size-fits-all yardstick. We rejected list-based morality drawn from religious traditions. Thus the yardstick we seek cannot be a one-dimensional "ruler" that we lay actions beside, rank according to a pre-ordained scale of goodness or badness, then use to beat the bad with while heroizing the good.

Rather, the moral yardstick we have found functions in two directions, outwardly and inwardly, in the realms of ethics and inner morality. Ethics pertains to our collective social interaction; inner morality pertains to our individual spiritual experience. Ethics aims to make the society in which we live a better place; inner morality aims to make each of us a better person. There are two overlaps between these two directions that unite them and show how they are two aspects of the one moral perspective.

The first overlap is revealed in the use of the word "better." Such usage assumes that the purpose of morality is to help us make our shared society a "better" one in which to live, while also individually making ourselves "better" people. Making our society a better place, in current Western secular terms, is developing the way our communities and countries function so that the liberal values on which they are established, including personal freedoms, democratic processes, political secularism, and cultural pluralism, can help our society develop into the best it can be for all citizens equally. Making ourselves better people involves developing ethically, from self-interested to all-embracing.

"Better" applies to inner morality in both an outward and inward sense. Socially, inner morality (as with ethics) requires each of us to become better citizens of the societies in which we live, similarly developing from being self-involved and self-justifying to practicing universalized moral attitudes. The inward goal of inner morality is to apprehend mystically. Becoming a "better" person in this sense involves using inner virtues to transform ourselves from ignorant and rule-bound, oppressed or oppressing, into someone who apprehends on a transcendent level of awareness.

Clearly, behind all these uses of the word "better" is the idea of social and personal moral growth. Morality does not hinge on the pugnacious application of rigid rules. Morality is not a static yardstick against which we measure ourselves. Rather, in its ideal sense, morality is an on-going activity which enables a society and its citizens to become "better."

The second overlap between ethics and inner morality is that both hinge on our shared humanity. Thus a "better" society involves establishing an environment in which all citizens equally have the opportunity to develop to their human potential. An unethical society oppresses, exploits, and harms its own citizens and the citizens of other societies. In comparison, an ethical society establishes social norms, laws, and customary practices that facilitate the growth of both its own citizens and the citizens of other cultures.

Thus becoming a "better" person involves not oppressing, exploiting, or harming others, developing from a self-involved to an expanded ethical moral outlook, and progressing towards the inner goal of mystic spiritual insight. Clearly, this growth also involves achieving our human potential, because whatever our social, intellectual, or transcendent spiritual perceptions, we remain human beings throughout. This is why the Buddha linked socially-directed ethical virtues to inwardly-directed wisdom virtues—because whether we are acting in the external social world or exploring the psycho-spiritual world within, we remain human beings living according to our human potential.

Given, then, that morality functions in these two directions, and on these various levels, it is possible to say now that the moral yardstick we have been seeking is three-dimensional in scope. These three dimensions consist of the social-physical, the conceptual-intelligible, and psycho-spiritual realms.

Together, these three realms encompass everything that is everyday and transcendent, worldly and mystic, mundane and extraordinary, which we experience as human beings. The moral impulse (however one sees it as being generated, whether genetically, socially, psychologically, rationally, or religiously) runs though all three realms equally, pushing us to better ourselves and providing us with the means, through the process of conscience and the practice of virtues, to contribute to the improvement of the world we are collectively making for ourselves.

Ultimately, as most of the thinkers examined in these pages have argued, we are autonomous moral beings. This means that we each have the freedom to exercise our individual moral choice. But as social beings, living with others, we also live with others. As J.S. Mill asserted, this involves having a responsibility not to harm others, and considering others who will be affected by whatever we choose to do. Simultaneously, and beyond the reach of our society's norms, customs and laws, we have to decide for ourselves what we consider to be morally acceptable and unacceptable.

A Sufi adage states that we should be *in* the world, but not *of* the world. Adapting this adage to this discussion, it could be said that morality involves acting ethically within the norms our society has established, but simultaneously expanding our perspective so that our moral sense is not wholly of our society. This means that we are always responsible for our own moral perspective. As the Buddha maintained:

PROPOSED MODEL FOR A MORAL YARDSTICK			
	SOCIAL-PHYSICAL	CONCEPTUAL-INTELLIGIBLE	PSYCHO-SPIRITUAL
ETHICS (Social interaction)	Making a "better" community	Universalizing all ethical decision-making	Enhancing each citizen's human potential
INNER MORALITY (Personal experience)	Making a "better" citizen	Practicing virtues of self-mastery	Enhacing each individual's inner potential

FIGURE 15.1

Do not be led by reports, or traditions, or hearsay. Do not be led by the authority of religious texts, nor by mere logic or inference, nor by considering appearances, nor by the delight in speculative opinions, nor by seeming possibilities, nor by the idea: "This is our teacher." But, O Kalamas, when you know for yourselves that certain things are unwholesome and wrong, and bad, then give them up. … And when you know for yourselves that certain things are wholesome and good, then accept them and follow them.[3]

Accordingly, we can now make a conclusion with respect to what a moral yardstick looks like that we can use in contemporary Western societies. This yardstick is not a thing. Rather, it is an on-going process that is never complete, the results of which can always be bettered.

Thus morality, as an on-going process, functions simultaneously in the three realms of the social, the conceptual, and the spiritual; requires us to rise out of our lowest, self-involved attitudes to the highest universalized outlook; necessitates the use of rational thought to examine and confront our own personal assumptions and those our society advocates; pushes us to identify virtues that we should practice and vices that we should stop carrying out; and enables us to realize the potential of what is deepest in us—our own humanity.

CHAPTER 16

What Is The Good In Human Existence?

We have arrived at what I hope is a clear view of what morality is and how it functions today. However, one issue remains to be examined. When I began this investigation, I acknowledged that while the good life, as defined by Zarathushtra, the Buddha, and Plato, aims to offer us the opportunity to achieve happiness, harmony, knowledge, fulfilment, and wisdom, in reality our world is complex, messy, inharmonious, and filled with suffering, ignorance, and stupidity. All of which makes it unlikely that we will collectively realize any concept of the ideal "good life."

There is no disagreement over the fact that across the globe inequalities in wealth, employment, education, and opportunity continue. War shows no sign of abatement. Fear and religious beliefs continue to be used to justify killing all around the globe. Meanwhile, the proportion of civilians to combatants being injured or killed during conflicts and wars rises globally. A free media, necessary to ensure citizens are informed and to monitor the performance of elected and non-elected rulers, is declining due to commercial pressures or state control. And profit wins out in many debates regarding sustaining the quality of all life. So while we human beings have a natural tendency to join together in order to achieve far more than we would as isolated individuals, the way we come together leads us to choose, in Zarathushtra's words, to build "houses of worst existence" rather than "houses of good purpose."

Morally we can say that our highest capacities are too often captured by our lowest, and that collectively and individually we struggle to realize the good in our lives. As the Sufi, Hazrat Inayat Khan, observed:

From the point of view of the mystic, a person in whom there is a balance of thought and sentiment, who is awakened to the feeling of

> another, and who is conscientious in everything he [or she] does and
> is aware of the effect that it produces on others, is beginning to be
> human. In other words, it is not an easy thing even for a man to be
> a man [or a woman to be a woman]. Sometimes it takes a life time.[4]

This, it could be argued, is the heart of our moral situation. We are moral beings—but in potential. We are human beings—but in potential. So how may we to transform that potential into reality? I have suggested that there are two aspects to our morality, which I have named ethics and inner morality. Are they sufficient, in themselves, to counter-balance the inhumane ways we treat each other?

Clearly, if the liberal freedoms that form the foundations of Western societies were fully understood and applied, then a more equitable, tolerant, compassionate, and just society would be established, without having to change the liberal premises that provide the moral basis of our lives. In addition, if all the world's citizens strove to develop their moral disposition by shedding their prejudices and intolerance, replacing them with expansive attitudes such as understanding and acceptance, then all societies would be in a far stronger position to realize their political, economic, spiritual, and human potential.

However, a number of forces embedded in our collective behavior clearly work against this urge to realize our human potential. One is ignorance, which results from lack of education, and from being caught up in a narrow view of the global village. Another is self-justification, which is so self-involved that it sets aside reason in order to continue doing what it wants to do. Self-justification, being closed, prevents growth. A third force is greed, a form of self-interest that is viewed as necessary for stimulating growth on the grounds that people will only improve anything if there is something in it for them. I will discuss this in the next section. The problem is, when greed is partnered with ruthlessness, extreme self-interest is brought to situations that is detrimental not only to all involved, but to the perpetrators' own humanity.

Self-interest is a natural, biologically ingrained, and socially reinforced impulse. It is a positive when balanced with sympathy and with an expansive outlook. But self-interest on the national, international, and corporate levels is arguably the greatest hindrance to humanity realizing its moral and human potential. Clearly, there is a need to balance self-interest with a rational, universalizing outlook if we are to become what we could be.

UNITIVE MORALITY

This brings us back to the question of what moral ideal we could, and perhaps should, live by. The competitive free market economic system by which we live today has many flaws. Naked self-interest, greed, and ruthlessness may be virtues in the corporate world. But few of us want to live entirely by them. Increasing numbers of ethically-inclined buyers and business people are striving to create markets that are responsible to those who grow and provide food, goods, and services, that acknowledge social costs, that are sustainable economically, and that are sensitive to environment impacts. So while greed, self-interest and ruthlessness have taken control in many parts of our lives, we know that they are not sustainable long-term. We need to balance them by giving back.

The Fourth Way teacher, G.I. Gurdjieff, considered that the world functions according to a principle he called "reciprocal maintenance." By this he meant that all actions involve an exchange, whether of energy, emotion, or thought. One scientific manifestation of this principle is in the first law of thermodynamics, which states that for every action there is an equal and opposite reaction. This seems simple, but in the world around us one reaction often leads to the creation of a chain of interlinked cause and effect. In horticulture, we know that planting vast areas in one crop draws concentrations of pests, which farmers combat with pesticides. These pesticides, such as dioxin, don't break down quickly so continue to exist after the crop has been harvested. They subsequently leach into the water table. Today dioxins have entered food chains all over the planet. Another example involves the act of reading this book. This book exists as a result of me putting my thoughts into words. But reading it requires you, the reader, to translate those words back into your own thoughts. Without this reciprocal exchange of thought, from me to the book, from the book to you, this book would be no more than sheets of paper marked by lines of ink. Relationships, learning, love, and raising children are each sustained by a continuous reciprocal process of giving, absorbing, and giving out again.

Reciprocal maintenance also applies to morality. In all our decision-making, we are engaged in on-going processes of absorbing information, making decisions, acting on them, receiving responses, re-processing, and giving out again. In this way reciprocal maintenance creates feedback loops which enhance—or diminish—the ethical and moral quality of our lives.

An interesting question now arises. I have concluded that morality exists on two levels, the socially and outwardly directed level of ethics, and the psycho-spiritual level of inner morality. Yet there is another level of our existence that neither of these two addresses. This is the level of the Earth on which we live. Beyond the Earth is the even more expansive realm of the whole cosmos.

The Earth may be viewed as an incredibly complex array of feedback loops, each sustained by reciprocal maintenance. Without these multi-layered feedback loops—geological, quantum, biological, chemical, environmental, communal—there would be no life on Earth. We certainly wouldn't exist to form societies or to develop individual perspectives on how we should live. Accordingly, by way of a conclusion, it would be useful to consider one last moral concept that acknowledges the way that we are all connected by innumerable links of reciprocal maintenance on the planetary level. I'll call this concept unitive morality.

Underpinning unitive morality is the premise that, in contradiction to Kant, each of us is not an entirely morally autonomous being. Instead, we need to acknowledge the degree to which we are physically, economically, socially, intellectually, morally, and spiritually tied to each other, and not just in communities, but on the planet which we all share. The great lesson of globalization is that we do not live in isolated villages, but that we are each participants in one vast tribe called humanity. And this tribe of humanity is but one species in a biologically linked activity we call life. So we need to develop a form of morality that places us as ethical beings existing in a relationship of reciprocal maintenance with and within the Earth's biosphere.

Thus where ethics has us face the society in which we live, and where inner morality has us face ourselves, unitive morality would have us face the reality of living on this planet. Where ethics is concerned with how we make decisions and act in our society, and where inner morality is concerned with the psycho-spiritual state we create within ourselves, unitive morality is concerned with the Earth of which we are each a tiny dependent, and contributing, part.

As with inner morality, unitive morality can be considered to function on the sensible, intelligible, and mystical levels.

On the sensual-sensible level, unitive morality has to do directly with the Earth. Ecological and environmental issues have recently come to prominence because of the impact human waste, de-forestation, over-fishing, interruption and decimation of food chains, mono-cultural agriculture, fresh water shortages, and changing climate are having on our lives. The way human beings have plundered the Earth's resources, decimated other species, unbalanced the Earth's natural state, and screwed up the environment for future generations, shows the extent to which a self-interested, profit-focused free market "me first" attitude is harming the planet on which we live. Unitive morality requires us to look beyond ourselves as a species to see the natural balances existing on the planet, and to make rational decisions conducive to living harmoniously with them in an ongoing and viable state of reciprocal maintenance.

On the conceptual-intelligible level, unitive morality has to do with the way we use thoughts. Today's globalized media enables a thought to travel around the world in minutes. Although, ironically, we rarely think about them, thoughts are incredibly significant in our lives. We view the world through the framework of our thoughts. We interpret what is going on around us through a variety of moral, amoral, or immoral pre-conceptions. We use thoughts to stimulate greed, fear, selfishness, prejudice, and hate. But we also use thought to promote acceptance, tolerance, understanding, compassion, and generosity. As the Buddha emphasized, by our thought we raise ourselves up, and by our thought we drag ourselves down. In Zarathushtra's terms, by our collective thought we build the House of Good Purpose, and by our collective thought we imprison ourselves in the House of Worst Existence. Thus on the conceptual-intelligible level, unitive morality requires us to expand our thinking, and to ensure that all we think contributes to our mutual reciprocal maintenance.

Finally, there is the transcendental spiritual reality that surrounds and penetrates us. People experience this reality in different ways, to a variety of degrees, thinking about it within different cultural perspectives. Many of us drink from it, some help us access it, others try to lay claim to it. Of course, it belongs to no one. No single saint, prophet, or religion can have a monopoly on the reality that transcends us. Like the air, it is all around us and in us, freely available every moment of our lives. Unitive morality encourages us to acknowledge the transcendent reality of which we are a part, however each of us defines that reality, and to give back to it through the activities of our own existence. In this way, at the centre of whatever form our spirituality takes, is an on-going act of reciprocal maintenance between our mortal selves and transcendent reality.

The single greatest vice with respect to unitive morality is ignorance, which reinforces narrow self-interest and self-involvement. Unitive morality's greatest virtue is humility, which helps us come to understand our collective and individual place in the world. Responsibility with respect to unitive morality derives from gratitude, and gratitude derived from the fact that we exist. Embracing unitive morality means adopting an attitude of grateful acknowledgment that we are guests on this planet, not the owners of it. Each one of us is here for a short time only. Being a good guest involves leaving the world at least in as good, if not better, shape than when we arrived.

BIBLIOGRAPHY

Al-Arabi, Muhyi'ddin Ibn (1978). *Tarjuman al-Ashwaq*. Translated by Reynold A. Nicholson, London: Theosophical Publishing House.

Aquinas, St Thomas, *Summa Theologica*.

Armstrong, Karen (1999). *A History of God*. London: Vintage.

Augustine of Hippo. *The Morals of the Christian Church*.

Azargoshasb, Mobed Firoz. *The Holy Songs of Zarathushtra*. Available on-line at www.zarathushtra.com.

Buddharakkhita, Acharya (1985). *Dhamapada*. Kandy: Buddhist Publication Society.

Boyce, Mary (1984). *Zoroastrianism*. The University of Chicago Press.

Brickhouse, Thomas C., and Smith, Nicholas D. (1995). *Plato's Socrates*. NY and Oxford: Oxford University Press.

Coppens, Charles (1909). *Examining a Conscience*. Originally published in *The Catholic Encyclopedia*, Volume V, New York: Robert Company. Available on-line: www.newadvent.org/cathen/0657a.htm. Transcribed by Joseph P. Thomas.

Darwin, Charles (1981, orig. pub. 1871). *The Descent of Man, and Selection in Relation to Sex*. Princeton: Princeton University Press.

Dawkins, Richard (1991). *The Blind Watchmaker*. London: Penguin.

Daniel C. Dennett (1996). *Darwin's Dangerous Idea: Evolution and the Meanings of Life*. London: Penguin.

De Waal., Franz (2006). *Primates and Philosophers: How Morality Evolved*. Edited by Stephen Macedo and Josiah Ober. Princeton: Princeton University Press.

Eisler, Raine (1988). *The Chalice and the Blade*. HarperSanFrancisco.

Fakhry, Majid (1997). *A Short Introduction to Islamic Philosophy, Theology and Mysticism*. Oxford: One World Publications.

Field, G.C. (1967). *Plato and his Contemporaries*. London: Methuen.

Finnis, John (2006). *Aquinas' Moral, Political, and Legal Philosophy*. SEP, (Spring 2006 Edition), Edward N. Zalta (ed.). http://plato.stanford.edu/archives/spr2006/entries/aquinas-moral-political/.

Gazzaniga, Michael S (2006). *The Ethical Brain*. NY: Harper Perennial.

Gimbutas, Marija (1991) *The Civilization of the Goddess*. Harper SanFrancisco.

Gowans, Chris (2004). *"Moral Relativism"*. SEP (Spring 2004 Ed), Edward N. Zalta (ed.). http://plato.stanford.edu/archives/spr2004/entries/moral-relativism/

Hick, John (1964). *The Existence of God*. NY: Macmillan Publishing Company.

Himmelfarb, Gertrude (1999). *One Nation, Two Cultures*. New York: Knopf.

Jafarey, Ali A. (1991). *The Good Religion and Institutionalized Zoroastrianism*. On-line: www.zoroastrian.org/articles/The_Good_Religion_and_Zoroastrianism.htm

Kaplan, Aryeh (1988). *Meditation and the Bible*. Maine: Samuel Weiser.

______ (1989). *The Bahir*. Maine: Samuel Weiser.

______ (1982). *Meditation and the Bible*. Maine: Samuel Weiser.

Khan, Hazrat Inayat (1973). *The Sufi Message of Hazrat Inayat Khan*. Volume VIII: Sufi Teachings. London: Barrie Jenkins.

Lewy, Hands (ed) (2004). *Selected Writings: Philo of Alexandria*. NY: Dover.

McEvilley, Thomas (2002). *The Shape of Ancient Thought: Comparative Studies in Greek and Indian Philosophies*. NY: Allworth Press.

Maimonides, Moses (1963). *The Guide of the Perplexed*. Translated by Shlomo Pines, Chicago and London: University of Chicago Press.

Maringer, Johannes (1960). *The Gods of Prehistoric Man*. London: Weidenfeld and Nicholson.

Mellaart, James (1967). *Catal Hüyük, A Neolithic Town in Anatolia*. London: Thames and Hudson.

Mill, J.S. (1863). *Utilitarianism*. London: Parker, Son and Bourne.

Mills, L.H (1974). *The Zend-Avesta* Part III. Motilal Banarsidass.

Naydler, Jeremy (1996). *Temple of the Cosmos*. Vermont: Inner Traditions.

Newburg, Andrew, Eugene D'Aquill, and Vince Rause (2002). *Why God Won't Go Away: Brain Science and the Biology of Belief*. NY: Ballantine Books.

Nicoll, Maurice (1955). *The Mark*. London: Vincent Stuart.

Osbourne, Arthur (ed) (1987). *The Teachings of Ramana Marharshi*. London: Century/Rider.

Ouspensky, P.D (1971). *The Fourth Way*. NY: Vintage Books.

Pinker, Steven (2003). *The Blank Slate*. London: Penguin Books.

Plato (1994). *Gorgias*. Translated by Robin A.H. Waterfield. Oxford University Press.

______ (1987). *Theaetetus*. Translated by Robin A.H. Waterfield. London: Penguin.

______ (1951). *The Symposium*. Translated by Walter Hamilton. London: Penguin.

Rickaby, John (1908). *Conscience, Part III: What is Conscience in a Man?* Originally published in *The Catholic Encyclopedia*, Volume IV, New York: Robert Company. Available on-line: www.newadvent.org/cathen/04268a.htm. Transcribed by Rick McCarty.

Stanford Encyclopedia of Philosophy, The. (On-line edition).

Shah, Idries (1969). *The Sufis*. London: Jonathan Cape.

Singer, Peter (1993). *Practical Ethics*. NY: Cambridge University Press.

Smith, Adam (1790). *The Theory of Moral Sentiments*. London: A. Millar. 6th ed.

Suzuki, Beatrice Lane (1972). *Mahayana Buddhism*. NY: The Macmillian Company.

Tahula, Walpola. *What the Buddha Taught*. Published by Buddhist Youth Accociation Ltd, China.

Underhill, Evelyn. *Mysticism*, New York: E.P. Dutton & Co, 1961.

Vivekananda, Swami (1982). *Raja-Yoga*. Calcutta: Advaita Ashrama.

Wallis Budge, E.A. (1998). *The Egyptian Book of the Dead*. NY: Dover.

Wilber, Ken (2001). *The Eye of the Spirit*. Boston: Shambhala (3rd ed).

______ (1996). *A Complete Theory of Everything*. Boston: Shambhala.

Wink, Walter (1998). *The Powers That Be: Theology for a New Millennium.* NY: Galillee/
     Doubleday.
Wright, Robert (1994). *The Moral Animal: Evolutionary Psychology and Everyday Life.*
     London: Abacus.
Zaehner, R.C. (1976). *The Teachings of the Magi.* NY: Oxford University Press.

NOTES AND REFERENCES

PART 1: THE GOOD LIFE
1   Azargoshasb, *Gathas*, Yasna 53.2. The obscurity of the language in which Zara-thushtra's *Gathas* are written makes it difficult to translate them, leading to significant variations between different translations.
2   Boyce, *Zoroastrianism*, pp 58 and 71 respectively.
3   Plato, *Gorgias*, translated by Waterfield, quoted in a note on 41e.

PART II: HOW DO WE DEFINE THE GOOD?
1   Augustine, *The Morals of the Christian Church*, see chapter 15.
2   Smith, *The Theory of Moral Sentiments*, Section 1, Chapter 1.
3   Himmelfarb, *One Nation, Two Cultures*, p 5.
4   See Gowans, *Moral Relativism*.
5   Ibid.
6   Plato, *Theaetetus*, translated by Waterfield, p 30.
7   *Catechism of the Catholic Church*, 416—418.
8   Mill, *Utilitarianism*, Chapter 2.
9   Singer, *Practical Ethics*, pp 11-12.
10   Ibid, p 14.
11   See http://en.wikipedia.org/wiki/Ayn_Rand.
12   For examples of new Darwinist thought see Dawkins, Wright, Dennett, Pinker.
13   Wright, *The Moral Animal*, pp 24—26.
14   Ibid, p 158.
15   Ibid, pp 146, 148, 208.
16   Aquinas, *Summa Theologica*, Q 94, Article 3.
17   Underhill, *Mysticism*, p 72.
18   Hick, *The Existence of God*, pp 223-224.
19   See Newburg, D'Aquill, Rause.
20   Quoted in Armstrong, *A History of God*, Udana 8.13.
21   Azargoshasb, *The Holy Songs of Zarathushtra*, Yasnas 45.8, 44.1, 43.2.
22   Plato, *The Symposium*, translated by Hamilton, pp 93-95.
23   Singer, *Practical Ethics*, p 6.

PART III: HOW DOES THE GOOD WORK IN OUR LIVES?
1   For an account of Kohlberg's work see the Wikipedia article at http://en.wikipedia.org/wiki/Kohlberg%27s_stages_of_moral_development.
2   Wilber, *The Eye of the Spirit*, p 170.

3   Mellart, *Catal Hüyük*, see plates 46-49.

4   Maringer, *The Gods of Prehistoric Man*, see pp 36 and 39.

5   Ouspensky, *In Search of the Miraculous*, p 149.

PART IV: IS THERE A GOOD TO STEER OUR LIVES BY?

1   Boyce, p 133.

2   Ibid, Yasnas 30.1–4 and 48.4, pp 35 and 39.

3   Suzuki, *Mahayana Buddhism*, quoted pp 123, 125 and 127.

4   Armstrong, p 144.

5   *The Literal Meaning of Genesis by Augustine of Hippo*, IX, V, 9, quoted by Armstrong, p 146.

6   Augustine of Hippo, *Enchyridion*, 26-27.

7   Gimbutas, *The Civilization of the Goddess*, p 396.

8   See Eisler, *The Chalice and the Blade*.

9   Wink, *The Powers That Be: Theology for a New Millennium*, p 39.

10 Ibid, pp 42-42.

11 Patanjali, *Yoga Aphorisms*, Discourse 2:30. Numerous translations are available.

12 All forty-two are listed on Wikipedia: http://en.wikipedia.org/wiki/Maat

13 Yasnas 45.8, 44.1, 43.2.

14 Buddharakkhita, *Dharmapada*, verses 153 and 154. According to Buddhist tradition these verses were the first words the Buddha spoke after his Enlightenment. Symbolically, the house refers to an individual's existence in samsara (the world of sense experience), the house-builder to desire, the rafters to the passions, and the ridge-pole to ignorance.

15 Kaplan, *Meditation and the Bible*, p 89.

16 See Lewy, *Selected Writings: Philo of Alexandria*.

17 For example, see Kaplan.

18 For more details see Fakhry, *A Short Introduction to Islamic Philosophy, Theology and Mysticism*.

19 See Suzuki.

20 Quoted in Naydler, *Temple of the Cosmos*, p 273.

21 Ibid, p 274.

22 Yasnas 51:13 and 31: 15, 20 , 21.

23 It is questionable whether Zarathushtra himself taught this. For a fuller exposition and quotations from relevant Zoroastrian literature, see Zaehner.

24 For a full discussion, including a thorough review of all evidences for the connection of Greek and Indian acceptance of the doctrine of reincarnation, see McEvilley, *The Shape of Ancient Thought*, pp 98 ff.

25 Ibid, p 98.

26 Hill, *Bhagavad Gita*, Discourse 9, verses 20-21.

27 McEvilley, p 99.

28 Singer, p 295.
29 Darwin, *The Descent of Man*, p 165-166.
30 Pinker, *The Blank Slate* , p 271.
31 Ibid, noted pg 271.
32 Ibid, p 272.
33 Gazzaniga, *The Ethical Brain*, p 169.
34 Ibid, p 171.
35 Quoted from Finnis, *Aquinas' Moral, Political, and Legal Philosophy*.
36 Peter Singer commenting in De Waal, *Primates and Philosophers*, pp 145-146.
37 Ouspensky, p 151.
38 From Coppens, *Examining a Conscience*.

PART V. ARE THERE LADDERS TO THE GOOD?
1 For a brief summary of the origins of the Zoroastrian religion, its historical development, and its current forms, see Jafarey, *The Good Religion and Institutionalized Zoroastrianism*.
2 Boyce, Yasna 30:2, pg 35.
3 Ibid, Yasna 48:5-12, pg 39.
4 Tahula, *What the Buddha Taught*, p 3.
5 Plato, *Gorgias*, section 488a.
6 Field, *Plato and his Contemporaries*, p 98.
7 From *The Shorter English Oxford Dictionary*, Oxford: Clarendon Press, 1977.
8 Field, p 103.
9 These six qualities and their descriptions taken from Jafarey.
10 This description of the Eightfold Nobel Path is largely taken from Tahula.
11 Tahula, p 49.
12 Brickhouse and Smith, *Plato's Socrates*, p 71.
13 Plato, *Theatetus*, section 176a-c.
14 Cleanliness includes not just physical cleanliness but also psychological cleanliness, particularly not indulging in self-involved negative emotions and attitudes. Contentment means practicing acceptance of our lot in life and eliminating such attitudes as dissatisfaction, resentment, and greed. Austerity involves learning to detach our awareness from the activity of the world that is constantly swirling around us and to practice turning our awareness inward. Study involves developing a philosophic outlook, and learning about the practices that underpin inner development. Surrendering the sense of self involves growing out of self-involvement and egotism, and replacing limiting and destructive attitudes with those virtues that facilitate inner growth.
15 Vivekanada, *Raja Yoga*, p 19.
16 Kaplan, p 194.
17 Ibid, p 195.

18   Ibid, p 183.
19   For an interesting discussion of metanoia see Nicoll, *The Mark,* pg 89 ff.
20   Osbourne, *The Teachings of Ramana Marharshi,* see pg 9.

PART VI. LIVING THE GOOD LIFE
1   Singer, pp 11-12.
2   Vivekananda, p 19.
3   Tahula, p 3.
4   Khan, *The Sufi Message of Hazrat Inayat Khan,* Vol VIII, p 29.

INDEX